WINNING ATTITUDES

IN THE FACE OF ADVERSITY

By

DAVID PASIPANODYA

Dedication

I would like to dedicate this book to those who have been here, those who are still here and those still to come.

To all those people worldwide who have passed on as a result of any form of cancer.

My special dedication goes to all those people who have survived all forms of cancer. To have shared the journey you walked in your mind, body and spirit was, for me, a privilege, honour and a great source of personal growth.

My other dedication goes to those facing any form of cancer, wellness challenge or whatever adversity. I trust that you will, on your journey, find time to reflect on your situation and be led just one first step up into an empowered tomorrow.

I also dedicate this book to my children Elizabeth, Tanaka, Tatenda, Tadiwa and Tarongerwa; my daughter-in-law Yolisa and my son-in-law Derek. Your love, care and respect have encouraged me to continue to dream. I hope in some way, my life and especially this book will encourage you to dream bigger and achieve more than I have in the past and will achieve in the remaining years of my life.

My final dedication goes to my grandchildren Tungamirai, Tirivashe, Anashe and Matida as well as those grandchildren and great grandchildren yet to be born. May the pages of this book give you a glimpse of my personality, my thinking and my mindset. May you be inspired to overcome your own life's adversities and to become the best that you were destined to be.

WINNING ATTITUDES

"A truly inspiring story of an amazing journey of how one man overcame his cancer and empowered his body to wellness through the power of his mind that can now help you transform, heal and even master your life."

- Dr John Demartini – International best-selling author of *The Values Factor*

* * *

A "winning attitude" is the pathway to our personal success, a life of abundance and becoming bigger than our problems. Through his own life experiences and overcoming cancer, David Pasipanodya enriches us with 8 key fundamentals to actually achieve this goal. A must read!

- Larry O'Sullivan, Author and Guest Speaker- *Client Service Excellence, the 10 Commandments* and *How is my Driving? Motivational tips for Success in Business and Life.*

* * *

David's account of his encounter with Cancer is a stark reminder of the random nature of life's challenges. His journey begins with the shocking diagnosis of his Prostate Cancer and takes the reader through various stages of concomitant trauma. With the utilisation of personal affirmations and the valuable tools acquired via his training as a Life Coach, David triumphs over this deadly health demon. A must-read for anyone facing a similar challenge or considering a career in coaching. At the very least, the reader will have received a pro bono Life Coaching Session."

- Joe Parker – Comedian & Entrepreneur

Published by:

Write-On Publishing

Write-On Publishing
59 Tom Brown Boulevard
Santareme, St Francis Bay. 6312
Tel: +27(0)422941023
frank@writeonpublishing.co.za
www.writeonpublishing.co.za

Edited By Frank Nunan
Book Design & Layout: Frank Nunan
Cover by: Puwai Mpofu

ISBN: 978-0-6399193-8-6

Contents

Foreword

I first met David in Sydney, Australia where he was a regular attendee of some of the functions where I spoke on my regular visits there. My closest encounter with him was in July 2010 during a weekend seminar of my signature programme "*The Breakthough Experience*". I clearly remember that he had a very powerful experience that opened his heart and moved him to tears.

Eight months later David was diagnosed with prostate cancer. It is quite inspiring to hear that he was able to turn his challenging experience with cancer into a blessing and an incredible source of meaning and growth. In the midst of an adversity David connected with who he truly was and chose a purposeful mindset as his main source of strength in his battle with cancer. Not only was he inspired to transform his challenge. He was also inspired to turn his experience into the book that you have in your hand right now.

I believe that whatever experiences you've had throughout your life serve as "feedback loops" to help you become clearer on what you'd love to dedicate your life to doing, being and having. From reading David's book it is clear to me that this was the purpose of his encounter with prostate cancer and he seems to have fully embraced this.

I also believe that the challenges you face are there for equilibration and serve a greater purpose; they are ultimately no mistakes. What you have perceived as your greatest obstacles are exactly what you needed to find out who you authentically are today and who you will be in the future. I urge you to be grateful for your challenges. By including a chapter on gratitude in his book David is clearly expressing deep gratitude for his cancer challenge. Whatever you're grateful for becomes fuel for your life's journey.

David's book is a truly inspiring story of an amazing journey of how one man overcame his cancer and empowered his body to wellness through the power of his mind that can now help you transform, heal and even master your life.

Dr John Demartini –
International best-selling author of
The Values Factor

INTRODUCTION

Your living is determined not so much by what life brings to you as by the attitude you bring to life; not so much by what happens to you as by the way your mind looks at what happens.
Bob Proctor

It was 5pm Sydney time on the 1st of March 2011. Before I had even sat down, my urologist tactlessly broke the news: "You have prostate cancer."

Totally unprepared, my immediate response was confusion. I got so confused I almost missed my chair as I tried to sit down. For a moment that seemed endless, I sat there with my mouth open, in a speechless daze.

After what seemed another eternity my unbelieving mind forced these lifeless words through my dry mouth: "What does that mean?"

The urologist then proceeded to show me a plastic model of the prostate and all the vital organs around it. He tried to explain the biology of it all and what could have triggered off the activation of cancerous cells. He might as well have been talking to himself.

What I still clearly remember him saying was: "You have a very aggressive type of prostate cancer with a Gleason Score of eight." The urologist further explained that a Gleason score of eight meant that the cancer had most likely spread to other organs of my body. I would have to undergo further tests to determine what other parts of my body had been invaded by the active cancer cells. It could be my lungs. It could be my bones. It could be my stomach. It could be anything.

I felt devastated, overwhelmed and scared to death. My mind went into a spin and a myriad of questions raced through my mind. "How advanced is this cancer? How far has it spread? How soon am I going to die? How much pain am I going to endure? How am I going to handle this? Why has God allowed this to happen to me?"

The next three days were the longest days of my life. Fear completely dominated my imagination. On the screen of my mind, I pictured the cancer, intimidating and overwhelming, as it loomed larger and larger. I saw my physical body growing smaller and smaller and eventually getting swallowed by the cancer. I suffered mental agony, sleepless nights, a lot of confusion, and anxiety.

Death had never appeared so close and real in my life before. I could feel it. I could touch it. I could smell it. I felt pinned to the wall in death's corner. I had nowhere to go.

The prostate cancer diagnosis was irrefutable proof that a seed of death had been planted in my body and was growing daily. I could feel cold chills running continuously through my body. I was literally shivering.

This was a situation I had not prepared for at all. At no point in my entire life had I ever entertained the possibility of being diagnosed with any type of cancer. Two of my siblings had died of cancer, but I had never placed myself in their situation. I had buried my head in the sand. I had thought and behaved as if it would never happen to me

Now the fact that two of my siblings had succumbed to cancer haunted me and drove me crazy. It brought the certainty of my own death much closer. Cancer certainly ran in the family and I was the next victim. I was now standing in the family cancer death queue. There was no escape.

As I faced what I thought was an inevitable death, I asked myself: "In the 63 years that I have lived in this world, did I do the best I could with everything I had? Did I live my life to the full? Did I use the time I was given in this world as best as I could?"

My answer to each of these questions was a definite "NO!" I did not at all feel fulfilled about the way I had lived my life. And, most significantly, I had not accomplished my life's goals and dreams because I had always thought there was plenty of time. I kept on procrastinating and behaving as if I was immortal and time would always be on my side. Now as I looked death in the face I saw this shocking truth - "There is no time!"

The reality hit me that there had never been enough time. The countdown of the hours and days of my life had started from the very day I was born. For some reason, I had adopted a laid-back perception of time. I felt and behaved as if there was no hurry in this world and that there was plenty of time to do whatever needed to be done. Although I had had some big dreams and goals, I had never treated them with any urgency.

I would think of a big dream or goal and get excited and enthusiastic about it for a short while. Then after a few weeks or at most a month the fire would start dying and soon the big dream would be all but forgotten. In most cases a new dream would come along, and my new excitement in it would automatically relegate the old dream to the background.

Now as I faced the biggest threat of my entire life and the possibility of dying soon from cancer, I looked back at the years I had left behind and I didn't like what I saw. My past was littered with too many unfulfilled and broken dreams. I had made countless promises to myself and not fulfilled most of them.

I didn't feel too happy with myself and if I were to die at that point, I would die a disappointed man. I had been good at coming up with big dreams but had fallen far too shot on follow-up and completion. I saw myself as a failure. Now I might never get another chance? This could easily be the beginning of the end. I had missed my opportunity boat and now death was here.

On the fourth day after my diagnosis I felt out of control. My fear-ridden mind was now running my life. I didn't look and feel good at all. I seemed to have lost a great deal of weight in less than a week. I had averaged about four hours of sleep a day during those five days. I looked at myself in the mirror. My face was scrawny, scared and lifeless. I felt dizzy, confused and I was definitely not thinking straight.

My feet felt hot and painful. There was so much negative energy in and around me. I did not like how I looked. I did not like how I was thinking. I did not like how I felt. I could not go on like this. I needed a much clearer mind. There was too much noise going on in my head and everything felt completely out of control. I had to make sound decisions about how I was going to navigate my way through this cancer challenge.

Then it dawned on me. I was a life coach. I had helped quite a few people navigate through their challenges. I had completely forgotten about this in the first five days after the shocking news of my diagnosis. Self-pity and a victim mentality had completely taken over my life.

I now remembered that as a life coach I had often encouraged my clients with these words from Epictetus: "It is not what happens to you that matters, but how you react to it."

I thought to myself, "If I were to tell my coaching clients right now that I have been diagnosed with an aggressive type of prostate cancer what advice would they give me?"

It became crystal clear in my mind that it was not so much the fact that I had been diagnosed with prostate cancer, but rather the mindset I chose to have that would determine the quality of my life. This thought shifted my perspective and perception quite significantly.

The time had come for the coach to walk his talk.

For the first time since the news of my diagnosis I realised that I had to empower myself emotionally and spiritually if I wanted to move forward.

Up until that point I had chosen to respond with fear, anxiety, worry, panic and a victim mentality. The result was hopelessness and helplessness.

Now for the first time since the news of my diagnosis, I felt a glimmer of hope that I might have a chance. I had briefly focused on the opportunities and possibilities that I had in that seemingly dark moment and I had found something to hold on to.

I felt empowered. I felt positive. I felt energised.

I realised that since my diagnosis I had been focusing my mind exclusively on the possibilities of death. I had empowered the cancer and in the process completely disarmed myself. But now I realised that it was all about me and not the cancer. I, and not the cancer, had to choose how I wanted to live my life from then on. I had to choose to give myself a fighting chance. The quality of life that I was going to live was going to be determined by how I chose to live my life, not by focusing on the fact that I had prostate cancer. My choice of mindset was the key. I had to adopt a positive attitude!

As I prepared to face the cancer and go through my treatment programme, I decided I was going to focus on and depend on two forces or relationships that I believed would help me. The first was my relationship with God and the second was my relationship with myself.

I am a Christian who believes that God is the underlying power behind my very existence. He embodies all that is good to me and provides me with the answers to all the complexities and uncertainties that I face in my life and in the world around me. My connection with Him is the most important relationship in my life. All other relationships come second. He gives meaning to my life.

In the first few days after the prostate cancer diagnosis I was battling to find meaning in my life. I felt scared, confused and lost in thought most of the time. However, once I was able to perceive a link between how I related to God and how I related to myself, I began to see more meaning and I felt encouraged, energised and inspired to want to go on. I realised that the attitude I had towards myself would significantly influence my attitude towards God. This attitude would also determine the quality of my life and how I handled life's inevitable challenges.

And so I decided that as I faced the greatest challenge of my life, I was going to focus and work on my relationship with myself and with God. These were the two most important relationships in my life. If I could understand myself and connect with who I was – especially with the leader in me – then I would also grow in my understanding of who God was and what role he played. And hopefully I would also be able to understand what he was trying to say to me through the prostate cancer challenge I was facing.

I felt strongly that it all started with my relationship with myself. How I saw myself, my own self-image and the attitude I adopted would determine my actions and the kind of impact they had on my own life and on the world around me. My decisions and actions were clearly indicators of whether I loved myself or not. They determined whether or not I was treating myself well.

This important relationship with myself would determine the quality of life I was going to have as I navigated my way through prostate cancer. I decided to choose what I now call "winning attitudes". As a student of personal development and life coach I had come up with a coaching programme that I had given the title: "Connecting with the leader in you."

I had thought of this programme because of a very strong conviction that I held. I had come to believe that inside me and inside everyone else was a leader. In order to live a meaningful life, I was certain that the most important human being I needed to connect with was myself. I had to connect with the leader in me. It was clear to me that most of us were not aware of it. It also became clear to me that even for those who were aware of it, many did not know how to actually connect with this leader inside and bring him out.

And so I came up with what I now identify as: "Eight keys to connecting with the leader in you". These eight keys were basically attitudes that I felt a person could use to face his or her challenges positively and courageously. I also called them "winning attitudes". They were a distillation of the wisdom I had learnt and reflected upon as a life coach and student of personal development.

It was these eight keys that I chose to embrace as I faced the greatest challenge of my life. I decided to use them as an opportunity to deal with the cancer in a positive way. Ironically, my cancer diagnosis became a case study opportunity, with me as the guinea pig. I was going to test these eight keys on myself. Even if I was going to die as I went through my treatment, these keys would help me to see a brighter side of the otherwise dark and depressing subject that cancer was. Maybe I would die with a more positive outlook or, better still, a smile on my face.

I felt that these keys or attitudes would best be expressed as affirmations – powerful, positive, personal present-tense statements that I would say to myself. I very strongly believe in affirmations and associate them with prayer, which has a very powerful positive influence on me.

For many years now affirmations have given and continue to give me a sense of ownership of whatever I desire to become, to do or to have. I say them to myself almost every day. They have become what I call 'my mindset makers'. They have helped me to positively influence the way I think and behave.

For this reason I have included in this book a set of affirmations at the end of each of the eight chapters covering the eight keys for "Connecting with the leader in you"

So, what were the eight keys that I came up with?

Key # 1. I am Unique.

Key # 2. I am my own best friend.

Key # 3. I embrace my beauty and magnificence.

Key # 4. I have a purpose.

Key # 5. I have potential.

Key # 6. I am bigger than my problems.

Key # 7. I live in abundance.

Key # 8. I choose an attitude of gratitude.

These eight keys are the winning attitudes that helped me face my prostate cancer and survive it. Five years have now passed since I celebrated victory over prostate cancer. Since then I have been going for tests every six months and I am still free from the cancer. I continue to enjoy very good health and very high levels of energy. I continue to live a life with meaning and purpose.

The eight winning attitudes provided me with a mind-set which helped me manage my own body, mind and spirit during the challenging eighteen months of cancer treatment. Since my fight with cancer, I have success-fully used the eight winning attitudes to face other life challenges I have experienced and continue to experi-ence. I have now become totally convinced that anyone can use one, more or even all of these attitudes to deal with whatever challenges life throws at them.

My prostate cancer survival has been the strongest inspiration for me to write this book. Since being told I was cancer-free eighteen months after my diagnosis, I have felt deeply challenged to share my experiences.

Since that freedom day, I have seen, read and heard of many other people who have been diagnosed with prostate and many other types of cancer. Sadly, most of them have passed on. I am still here and I often wonder whether if they had heard my story it would have made any difference at all. Maybe I am still here because God wants me to tell my story and to share my experience.

I have become increasingly convinced that sharing my prostate cancer experience, as I am doing in this book, could have made some positive difference in the lives of some of those who have died from it. I might not have given them life itself, but maybe they would have come to the end of their lives with a more positive mindset. Therefore, I wrote this book as fast as I could in the hope that my own shared experiences might make a positive difference to other people's lives. I feel deeply relieved that I am not carrying my experience to my grave.

The other inspiration for me to write this book has to do with leaving a legacy. I have children and grandchildren and I am certain I will have many more grand- and great-grandchildren many generations after I have passed on. I am sure that many, if not all of them, would want to know who I was.

I often feel a burning desire to know who my father and mother really were. What really went on in their minds and in their lives? How I wish they had left something in writing. I would also love to know who their parents and grandparents were. But there is a deafening silence from their graves. They left nothing in writing and I sometimes feel sad about that.

Therefore I feel strongly inspired to leave something for my own children and grandchildren. Through this book I am certain that they will know who I was and what went on in my mind. I'm happy to be leaving a legacy.

In the pages that follow I am going to be focusing on and sharing with you my experiences with those eight keys and how they helped me survive the greatest challenge I have ever faced in my entire life. I will be sharing about my relationship with myself and how being able to connect with the leader in me helped me as I faced prostate cancer.

You don't have to read this book following the sequence in which the chapters have been presented. You can start with any chapter that interests you and still get something of value. Of course, you can also follow the sequence in which the chapters are arranged. It's all up to you.

In this book, I'm not suggesting at all that if anyone with cancer adopts the winning attitudes that I used, they will overcome the cancer. My book is not a medical prescription. It is not about how to treat cancer. I am not at all saying one form of treatment is preferable to another. It is about choosing a mindset that I believe will make a positive difference, whatever one's choice of treatment is. It is about adopting winning attitudes irrespective of the outcome of one's challenging situation.

Above all, in this book I'm sharing my own journey with cancer. I am sharing with you attitudes that I adopted that I believe made a positive psychological difference in my life from the time I first battled with cancer up until today.

I believe that my story is not only relevant for people who have had or will ever have prostate or any type of cancer. Whatever life challenge you have faced, are facing right now or will ever face, this story is also for you.

I also believe that my story is not just about challenges. It is also about connecting with who we are and finding meaning and purpose in our lives. It is about finding inner peace and connecting with the leader who resides within each one of us. It is also about the dreams and goals that each one of us has. It is about creating the right attitudes within us that will enable us to focus on and achieve those goals and dreams that are part of our destiny.

CHAPTER 1

I AM UNIQUE

"You were born an original. Don't die a copy."
John Mason

Unique and packaged for success
You landed in this big world
With an assignment uniquely yours
With gifts and talents no one had
In exactly the same way you had them

You look at yourself and then someone else
You look at them and think they're better
You curse yourself believing no better
Just stop it, don't even go that way
You're the one and only you

In this whole world with its billions
You've no compare, you stand unique
What you think and how you think
What you do and how you do it
Can only be done by the only you.

The world is fortunate, that it has you
What you contribute is unique to you
What you produce has only your prints
Its feel and touch and taste and smell
Has the signature of the only you
You stand as one, one of a kind

You are a one life gift to this world.
Make your stay here unique and impressive.
Make a difference that outlives you
Live out your unique mission and purpose
Let your gifts and talents be your footprints
That will speak of you when you're gone

My prostate cancer diagnosis created the biggest emotional and spiritual confrontation of my entire life. Emotionally, I experienced mixed feelings of anger, fear and disconnection. The fear of death that I initially had was so overwhelming that I felt emotionally numb with disbelief.

Reality was blurred for a while and I felt more comfortable in a make-believe world where I convinced myself I was dreaming. Although that wish and feeling was unsustainable I preferred it to reality. The thought of impending death literally stopped my thinking process. My mind just could not entertain the reality of death at such a short notice. I absolutely had no idea how to handle the truth.

When I could no longer mentally hide from the truth I felt defeated and ready to give up. I felt totally exposed and victimised. And surrendering to this victim mentality did not, at all, bring peace to my mind and spirit. Instead it opened a whole new world of torment. I now started thinking of how I was going to die.

I now began to imagine myself going through that endless agonising pain that I had seen on the suffering faces of so many cancer victims. I clearly recalled morphine being introduced to their treatment dosages to ease the pain and how I would see them lifeless, lying there and waiting to die. And by the time they died they were just skin and bones, a skeletal shadow of their former selves. That is what I pictured myself going through. And it sent chills down my spine.

One of the very first questions I asked after I had been told I had prostate cancer was directed at God. "Why? Why, God? Why me?" For quite a while I was angry with God and vented my anger every day. "I am a good Christian. I go to church every Sunday. I read the Bible and pray almost every day. Why have you allowed this to happen to me? What have I done to deserve this?"

I had enjoyed good health for so many years that I had begun to take God's protection for granted. In my entire 63 years in this world I had been hospitalised only once. And that once had not been because I was sick. I went in for a small operational procedure to remove a benign growth in my body. For all those years my clean bill of health had made me behave as if I had an irrevocable pact with God. I had assumed that I would be protected from any serious health issues for the rest of my life. I was shocked by the prostate cancer diagnosis. I was violently flung out of my comfort zone and realised that I was not as protected as I had thought I was. In fact, I felt seriously let down.

I searched my mind and my entire 63 years of life for the big sin I had committed that had earned me what I thought was the biggest curse any human being could be punished with. I was at first totally convinced that the cancer I had was retribution for something I had done wrong. However, my search never yielded any sin big enough to warrant death by cancer.

I felt as if I had been painted with a cancer colour that made me look and feel different from everyone else. It was as if I no longer belonged to the world of the living. I felt a physical, spiritual and mental isolation. I felt that people now saw me differently and that to them I was no longer normal. I believed that being diagnosed with cancer was a statement of notice that my days in this world were numbered. I felt that the diagnosis had made me a focus of pity and sympathy. I was alone and I wondered what people were thinking about me. Were they still seeing me as they had before? I doubted it. I felt like an outcast. I felt like a victim.

I increasingly believed that people were being nice to me out of politeness and pity. Everyone who knew about my cancer status was also seeing my death as a certainty. And therefore, they were feeling sorry for me and wondering how I was going to manage my impending last painful moments in this world.

I felt depressed, abandoned, ostracised and isolated. Whenever my thinking followed this track I would get so angry with God and end up asking the fruitless question "Why me?"

It was only when I began to reflect on my unique identity that the answers began to fall into place. I realised that those questions had arisen because I was comparing myself with other people. I was subconsciously looking at other people whose lives seemed okay and cancer-free and then asking God "Why me?" By its very nature, this question was accusing God of picking on me. By asking this question I was also suggesting that prostate cancer should not happen to me but to other people. "Why me?" implicitly meant "Why not someone else?" The question "Why me?" became my conduit and gateway to reconnecting with my unique identity.

I became aware that I lived in a world in which I was surrounded by people – in my family, at work, at church, everywhere I was. From a very young age, I had been subconsciously socialised to compare myself with the people around me. Comparing myself with other people determined whether I considered myself successful or not. This process of socialisation slowly submerged the consciousness of my unique individual identity. I lost my appreciation of this special person that I was supposed to be. Other people's lives and agendas took over my life. As I grew older, I completely lost touch with the fact that I was a unique person with unique talents through which I was supposed to express the unique purpose for which I had been born.

My reflection led to an introspective conversation with myself. It resulted in a monologue out of which emerged the answer to my 'Why me?' This monologue silenced forever the voice of the victim in me:

"This particular prostate cancer experience is unique and exclusive to me. No one has ever experienced it, is experiencing it now and will ever experience it at any time

in the future in the same way that I am experiencing it. Other people have experienced cancer before and are experiencing it now. But their experiences are unique to who they are. They have made their own choices about how they are going to deal with it. This is my freedom space and I am going to exercise my freedom of choice. I am going to make my own unique choices.

"What unique choices am I deciding to make in response to my cancer diagnosis? Am I deciding to make negative unique choices or positive ones? If I make negative choices, how is that going to help me? How is that going to affect my life now and in the future? What would the difference be if I made my own unique positive choices?

"I would rather make positive choices. In fact, I am making a choice to face this cancer with a positive mindset. My unique identity is giving me the option of choosing a uniquely positive response. This cancer experience is giving me an opportunity to make a choice that has my unique stamp of approval."

This certainly was not the victim's voice that had dominated my thinking since the news of my diagnosis. This was clearly the liberator's voice that had crafted and pronounced my declaration of independence. I felt empowered hearing that voice and I was very excited to encourage it and to give it room to grow.

I realised that I had a unique identity, separate from the specialists and all the other medical personnel who were going to be involved in my treatment. While I was going to co-operate with them as much as I felt was necessary, the ultimate decision about what I was going to do and how far I was prepared to go would depend on me as a unique individual, separate from every one of those people. My destiny was unique to me and was going to depend on what my attitude was going to be. I could choose my attitude and the choice was very simple – either positive or negative. Whatever choice I made, the implications would be far reaching.

By the time I was diagnosed with prostate cancer I knew that I was a unique individual. I knew that of the more than 7 billion people in the world, I was one of a kind and I was truly special. What I did not know, however, was that my unique identity would have any relevance in the face of a crisis of this nature. I certainly did not know that the crisis I faced would give me such an empowering confirmation of my unique identity.

I realised for the first time ever that my unique identity gave me an enormous amount of power. Only I was going to decide what quality of life I was going to have between that moment and whenever I was going to die. It could be long. It could be short. The realisation that I had the power to uniquely influence that time-space was both mind-blowing and very empowering. I didn't know when I was going to die and I still don't know. That time-space could be anything from a few hours, a few days, a few years or many years. However, I had this life-changing realisation that I could actually choose how I wanted to live the time-space that preceded my death.

Both the choice I made and my experience of it would be unique to who I was. The motivation and emotion surrounding my choice would not be anything that anyone else had ever experienced or would ever experience with the same intensity as I did. No-one else would ever connect with my "why" and the feelings that came with it as my unique self. Whatever choice I made was going to be coloured by my own unique background, past experiences and chosen values.

I became aware that whatever choices I was going to make regarding the prostate cancer, these choices would have consequences. Those consequences would impact my life as personal experiences that I would go through. And because my choices were unique to who I was, so would my experiences and consequences be unique.

Embracing my unique identity was for me a licence to be free. Comparing myself with other people was giving those people power over me. Whether I saw them as superior or inferior to myself, I was making them a yardstick of my life. My life could only derive meaning from an assessment of how I fared compared with them. I was suggesting that without them my very own identity was incomplete. It was quite a revelation to realise that I did not have to compare myself with anyone. I was free and complete as I was and no other person could add or take anything away from my unique identity. My unique identity gave me the freedom to be me and no one else.

The time-space that I occupied as I lived my life was unique to me. It was my time-space. Only I could fill that space, and the quality of life I chose as I moved in that space was entirely up to me. No one else would experience that quality of life in exactly the same way I would.

And the irony of it all was that my unique identity only made sense when I reflected it against a background that was made up of other people. I was not unique in my own secluded world. There were people around me. I was unique and different from each of my six brothers and two sisters. I was different from my wife and from each of our five children. I was different from any of my friends.

I realised that from the time I was born my goal had been to emulate and be like other people. As I grew up I developed a habit of always using other people as a point of reference. After all, most of what I had learned I had modelled from what I had observed other people doing as I grew up. All that I knew and did, from speaking, walking, eating, laughing and all other skills and habits, were things I had acquired from other people directly. I either saw other people and copied what they were doing until I got it or other people taught me. I had been trained to focus on other people and to learn and trust how they behaved. My interpretation of all this was that they were better than me. They mattered and I did not matter.

This kind of thinking had led me to focus on my limitations instead of my strengths. I saw myself falling short of the ideal I had in my mind and that I had based on other people. I actually had nothing to offer. This did not give me much self-confidence and as a result I had developed a poor self-image. It disconnected me from the value of who I was.

It was quite liberating for me to become aware that no other human being except myself had access to, and power and authority over the mindset I chose to adopt. I felt secure and empowered, knowing that I could create my own inner world that had the power to shape how I wanted to live. I could choose to aggressively control my situation and take full charge of how I was going to deal with the prostate cancer verdict that had been passed on me. I could also choose to completely surrender and resign my life to the cancer that had invaded my life. No one else needed to occupy that space and no one else needed to know the intimate details of that space.

I felt empowered, realising that my life and death were experiences unique to me. I had to live my own life as me and not as someone else. And this was all up to me. I had to make a choice, even if it was a choice no one else had ever made before. For the first time ever in my entire life I became aware of the tremendous power I had. I discovered an amazing power in just being me and nobody else. I had the freedom to choose. I had the freedom to be me. I was unique.

I realised that comparing myself with other people had not given me the energy and desire to improve my life. Instead it did one of two things: I would either feel complacent if I saw myself as better than someone else or I would feel inferior and inadequate when I focused on someone being better than me. Embracing my own unique identity helped me become aware that I was my own best yardstick. Comparing and assessing my present situation with where I was before and where I would like to be, helped me to strive to do better.

My experience with prostate cancer had no comparison. I knew that hundreds of thousands of other people throughout the entire world had experienced the very same prostate cancer I had been diagnosed with. However, the minute details of the circumstances of my experiences were uniquely different from those other thousands of people. I didn't have to adopt their attitudes and responses to their prostate cancer. As a unique individual, I refused to be intimidated by other people's experiences. I had the right to refuse to be influenced by their circumstances, their thinking, behaviour and destinies. These were all different from mine.

At first, I felt really scared when I remembered that my two brothers, Charles and Edward, had died of cancer. Their deaths had been traumatic experiences for me and I still vividly remembered their funerals and the great sense of loss that I felt then. The fact that there was this cancer history in the family reinforced my initial feeling of doom and gloom. Even before my diagnosis, it meant that my chances of dying from cancer were very high. The diagnosis had now sealed my fate. My doctor had told me that since my two brothers had died from cancer I had a very high chance of dying from it as well. My death was imminent. I saw myself as the next cancer casualty in the family.

However, as I focused more and more on my unique identity, it struck me that I was also uniquely different from each of my late brothers, Charles and Edward. The time, place and circumstances of their diagnoses were different from each other. Charles had died in his late fifties and Edward in his eighties. Maybe I was going to live until I was 90 or even 100. I believed that my own time, place and circumstances were different from theirs. God's plan for my life was different from theirs.

I asked myself "What if I decide not to believe that I would die of cancer because my two brothers had died of it? What if I decide to look that belief in the face and say NO! I am unique and I can do that! I wonder what would happen if I made those choices."

As I reflected on my unique difference to my two late brothers, I felt challenged to make an act of faith. I felt challenged to ask myself this question: "If you really believe you are unique and you don't want to die now, why don't you claim your time on earth?" And my response was this prayer and declaration: "I am praying for and claiming 35 more years." This has become a regular prayer and conviction for me. Because of my unique identity, I believe that it is possible.

I chose to believe that I could never live in any other person's world. Besides circumstances, my feelings, thoughts and actions were also different from other people even though we might have been facing similar challenges. More empowering for me was the option that became increasingly available to me – I had the freedom to choose to be positively different from other people. My unique identity gave me that power.

I found no cause to boast that I was dealing with this challenge better than anyone else. I also had no reason to bemoan my situation and complain about other cancer victims who seemed to be faring better than I was at the time. I was experiencing extremely uncomfortable hot flushes from the hormonal injection that was a major part of my treatment. Uncontrollable and embarrassing streams of sweat would break out on my face at any time, anywhere and in any situation. Initially I felt anxious and stressed by this situation. I saw myself as a victim and felt sorry for myself. Why was this happening to me and not the other cancer patients I was meeting every day?

It did not take me long to realise that this was happening to me because I was not the other cancer patients I was comparing myself with. This was my own unique experience, taking place at that unique moment during the space occupied by the gift of life that I had before I died – whenever I was going to die. I felt challenged to make the best of this space. I faced the choice of either seeing myself as a victim or a victor. I began to look at the hot flushes experience as a passing phase. Even though I felt uncomfortable, I chose to make the experience as positive as possible. And with time I got used to it and I felt less embarrassed. It was just a part of my treatment journey and it too would become a thing of the past.

As I read more and more about individuals who had faced cancer and survived, I realised that each person's experiences were unique. Each person had relied on their own unique inner strength.

One other important realisation I had was that the cancer and life journey I was walking was unique and exclusive to me. It had always been. I just had not awakened to it. No other human being understood the emotions and physical discomforts I was going through in exactly the way I was experiencing them.

Even if I were to explain to them as clearly as I could, they would never experience them as I did. They could just imagine. After all, they didn't really have the prostate cancer that I had.

No other human being could fully empathise with the fears, frustrations, anxieties and worries I was going through. At times, I was quite angry and frustrated with other people for not fully understanding my feelings about my situation. Then it dawned on me that they were actually doing their best and I should be appreciative of their empathy. The only human being who understood exactly what was going on was me. I was unique, and the sooner I used this to empower myself on this challenging journey I was travelling, the better.

The more connected I became to my unique identity, the more I felt empowered to think and act in ways that I had not heard anyone else thinking and acting. I was unique, and so I didn't have to follow anyone else. As long as I felt comfortable doing something, I felt encouraged to do it. My unique identity made me more daring to do things that I didn't know anyone else had done. Whether anyone else approved of it was not important. My own unique approval was sufficient for me to take action.

This also helped me, quite significantly, to think and act more independently and not just agree to everything that was being suggested to me about my treatment program. Embracing my unique identity empowered me to take total responsibility for my situation and to feel free to say no to suggestions regarding my life and health that I did not feel comfortable about. Fortunately, this did not turn me into an arrogant person. I just became more confident and cautious.

It was also quite a revelation to realise that my connection with God was unique. My knowledge and understanding of God was not the same as anyone else's. Because I have never entered anyone else's mind, even my wife's, I didn't know exactly what image they have of God. That meant that my relationship with him was very personal and unique and so was my faith in him. Through my prayers I had a unique access to his ears and heart. I believed that only God had unique and intimate access to who I was deep down inside.

I realised that besides my God I was the only one who had this unique and intimate access to the inner me. It was an "inner me" with a door which only I could open. I was the only human being who knew the combination that opened the lock to "inner me". As long as I was comfortable with who I was, nothing else mattered. This gave me a tremendous feeling of security. My unique identity and wellbeing were safe with me.

The most significant lesson I learnt from this experience is that your unique identity means nothing at all until you claim and embrace it. Until you value it, it remains valueless.

Recognising and embracing my unique identity has also made me more daring and adventurous. I am much less afraid to be me and I definitely don't need as much approval from other people for what I do as I used to. I no longer worry as much as I used to about what other people think of me. How I feel about me now matters more than how others feel about me. I just have to be totally comfortable with how I feel, think and do things.

My unique identity has become a source of freedom. I feel lighter now that I no longer tie other people's opinions and identities around my mind and carry them on my shoulders. At the same time, I have stopped blaming other people and circumstances for the way my life is. I have greater responsibility and only I have the power to change my circumstances.

Connecting with my unique identity has significantly helped me to totally acknowledge and accept myself as I am and not wish that my life was different from what it actually is. I realised that wishing my life was different puts me in a state of disconnection with who I am and upsets the resonance and peace with myself that I am supposed to enjoy. I saw and still see it as tantamount to saying to myself 'I shouldn't be here' when in actual fact I am here.

The present moment and my present identity are all I have. They are here. The past and the future only exist in my mind. They are memories and dreams which I can never make part of my "now".

I now believe that it is worth the time and effort to focus, mentally and emotionally, on learning to accept and be at peace with my status quo. I focus my mental and emotional effort on finding love, gratitude, joy and fulfilment in the way my life is. In this way, I can avoid the emotionally draining vicious cycle of remorse and regret

I now acknowledge the challenges I experience as

being unique to me. I no longer waste time asking "why" when things go wrong. I am more aware now that my unique challenges are meant to strengthen me and build me up as I travel my unique life's journey to my unique destiny. My challenges and destiny have no equal.

I now listen to myself more than I listen to other people. After all I spend more time with myself than with anyone else. This has given me greater self-awareness. I value who I am and I feel more connected to who I am. Once I am convinced that this is the unique and genuine me, I am no longer afraid to express who I am.

A good example of this has been in my public speaking journey. I have been a member of Toastmasters International since October 2011. In February 2014, I discovered that I could actually compose and sing my own songs! I felt totally fascinated and thrilled by this new gift and talent. I felt completely liberated spiritually and emotionally whenever I was composing, singing and writing my own motivational and spiritual songs. I still do.

Because of the freedom of self-expression that I felt through my songs, I wondered how it would be if I introduced my songs into my speeches. Since I felt so connected to myself while composing and singing my songs, I wondered whether I would not feel more connected to the people I was talking to by singing during my speech. I figured out that by doing so, my audience would also feel and experience the joy, energy and enthusiasm that I felt as I sang. The more I thought about it the more convinced I was that this would also be a more effective way of communicating my message to my audience.

In my three years with Toastmasters I had never seen, live, anyone singing during their speeches. So when I first thought of the idea, I felt uneasy, uncertain and scared. The fear, doubt, worry and anxiety that I felt were so strong that I initially dismissed the idea. Who was I to do something that no one else was doing?

Just as I was about to throw the idea out through the window I remembered a video I had watched of a lady who sang during her speech. This was at one of the Toastmasters International Public Speaking Contest finals. She won that contest and became the Toastmasters Public Speaking world champion for that year. She had a rare disease that resulted in her death not long after winning the contest. She became my source of inspiration. If, despite her medical condition, she could do it, I could do it too.

Thinking of that lady brought back the memories of my fight with cancer and how I had embraced my unique identity and won. So I decided that I was going to speak and sing because that's who I was – a unique individual who felt totally connected to myself through singing my own songs. I was choosing to bring some of my songs into my speeches and in that way express who I was and what I thought about life.

And so I tried it. It worked like magic. I felt more connected to myself and to my audience. Once again my unique identity had won the day.

Affirmations: I AM UNIQUE

- *Of the 7 billion people in the whole world I am one of a kind.*
- *I was born an original. I am not a copy of anyone.*
- *I am unique and therefore incomparable.*
- *What happens to other people doesn't have to happen to me.*
- *I am working on becoming a better person today than I was yesterday*
- *I have unique gifts talents and abilities.*
- *I am enough and I accept myself as I am.*
- *No one else can do what I can do in exactly the way I can do it.*
- *I am making a positive difference in the world in my own unique way.*
- *I have a unique purpose in this world that only I can fulfill.*

CHAPTER 2

I AM MY OWN BEST FRIEND

"The best day of your life is the one on which you decide your life is your own. No apologies or excuses. No one to lean on, rely on, or blame. . . you alone are responsible for the quality of it. This is the day your life really begins."
Bob Moawad

When no one's around and you're all - all alone
In the dark world of loneliness cold as a stone
Only listening to the dark mind's unspoken words
The only meaningful conversation your mind holds
Is the deep sigh and regret of no company and no friends

It's more devastating when personal challenge arises
And you only have loneliness as company in the crisis
Other people have heard, they know and sympathise
But what more can they do even if they are that wise?
Wrapped up and suffocating in their own challenges

Thinking about their own life is a full-time occupation
They have worries and concerns about their situation
They cannot take full charge of your 'big' challenge
Whose answers and solutions only you can arrange
Whose origins and complications only you can unravel.

The more you seek for help the more you feel alone
The more you seek for friends, the more you feel forlorn
Your nights are long and lonely - your mind is troubled
Morning comes and the mirror shows a face so humbled
The only face, your only company for this troubled day

Wait a minute mirror. Whose face is that? Looks so familiar.
My miraculous mirror has daily persisted. How peculiar?
That I search for companionship in the face of challenges
And I've missed the closest companion that life arranges
My own best friend who's always been there from day one

Who knows my life – challenges included - more than I do?
Who has better answers to my life's questions more than I do?
There's no greater hero who fights my battles more than I can
There's no greater encourager who inspires me more than I can
There's no one out there to motivate me better than I can

My own best friend, my closest companion, my lifetime gift
How I missed your presence, lost awareness and went adrift
Now that you're here my life's challenges I no longer fear
Tomorrow and the way forward are now so bright and clear
How warm it feels to converse with and embrace your presence.

L iving with cancer can be a very lonely experience, especially because of the stigma attached to it. Every cancer diagnosis is like a death sentence. The so-called medical experts at times even tell you how long you have left to live. Even if they don't tell you how long you have left to live you feel as if your death is imminent.

I felt estranged and distant from myself. I felt bad about me because I did not like myself with prostate cancer. I was not embracing me because I had cancer. I saw myself as a person with a very serious kind of disability. I felt disabled and prevented from planning for a future. I had no future. I was condemned to die soon. All my dreams were dead. Why would I entertain dreams about the future when I had been told I had stage four prostate cancer?

For almost a week after my diagnosis I was generating a lot of negative energy. I experienced frequent bouts of depression. I was generally grumpy and my level of appreciation hit rock bottom. I felt angry most of the time - with God, with other people and with myself. I was not in a good place. I didn't like where I was.

What had gone wrong with me? What on earth was I doing? What space was I getting myself into? Why was I allowing this huge blanket of negativity and depression to cover my life like this? How was I benefitting from being frequently sad and depressed? Was this how it felt to be diagnosed with cancer? How was such an attitude going to help me effectively deal with the prostate cancer challenge that I faced? How was this way of thinking empowering me?

These questions became my wake-up call and my lifeline. They challenged my whole victim mentality which was fast becoming the normal way of thinking for me. They brought me back to the level of positive awareness. They made me connect with who I was. And that is where I needed to be.

As a life coach and student of personal development, I should have known better. The more time I spent feeling all negative and depressed, the lower my immune system sank and the more of a field day the cancer cells in my body would have. I was actually being my own number one enemy. I was collaborating with the enemy. I was self-destructing.

Why was I giving away my birthright and not loving myself? Why was I surrendering responsibility in the most meaningful and important area of my precious life – relationships? Why was I turning my back on the most important person and relationship in my life – me and the relationship with myself? I was not loving myself at all.

I was building a growing list of what I wanted other people to do for me. As the list grew, so did my resentments because people were not coming to the party and meeting my expectations. I quickly concluded that they did not like me. Why would they like a person with cancer? I no longer added any value. I was just a liability.

My level of self-pity was so high that I expected people to drop what they were doing and sympathetically focus on me and my prostate cancer. I was projecting my own self-pity onto my wife, children and other people who were close to me.

Of all the people in my life, my wife bore the brunt of the high expectations that I had about what other people should do for me. My cancer diagnosis sent my expectation levels sky high. She had to be there one hundred percent for me. I made her responsible for my happiness.

For the thirty-six years that we had been married I had been quite emotionally dependent on her. I judged whether I was a good or bad guy based on whether she was validating me or not.

When she said I was doing great and she loved me I felt fantastic. And when she was not happy with what I had done or not done and criticised me I felt awful. I was even resentful of constructive criticism. I thought love was all about, being validated, appreciated and verbally praised by my wife.

I spent many years on this emotional roller coaster until the time of my cancer diagnosis. Initially I had very high expectations of her. Now that I was a "cancer patient" and "victim" I expected her to drop everything she was doing and focus on me.

I expected her to give me full-time sympathy especially as she was the only other person that I lived with. My cancer status became a convenient excuse for me to make my wife responsible for the quality of my life, in addition to her own life. But then my plan hit a snag.

At the time of my diagnosis my wife was in her final year of studies for a degree in Western Herbal Medicine. Unfortunately for me, she was in the middle of a heavy study program. On two or three days of the week it was not uncommon for her to be reading throughout the night until five in the morning. She would then have a shower and go off to college.

As much as I wanted her to be there for me when I needed her, she was not available. It would clearly not be fair of me to make demands on her time. With the heavy schedule that she had, I actually felt empathy for her.

With her out of the picture for most of the day and even the night as well, who else would be there for me as I confronted the greatest challenge of my life? My wife was the only other person who could validate me and had done so for 36 years. But now she was not available at the time that I needed her most.

None of our children lived with us anymore. Who else was going to be there for me twenty-four hours a day seven days a week to help me through this challenge? We were living in Sydney, Australia more than 15 000 kilometres from our African home. We had no close friends. Apart from our two daughters who were both married, we had no close relatives. We were isolated. I felt the brunt of it more than my wife did. I was clearly standing on my own and for a while I felt alone, unsupported and vulnerable.

Fortunately, I was not sitting idly at home and twiddling my thumbs. I had a nine-to-five job. I was still going to work even after the prostate cancer diagnosis . I commuted to and from work five days a week. I had a lot of time to think. I actually had a lot of conversations – with myself. I was asking myself a lot of questions and I was coming up with a lot of answers. At first my questions and answers were quite negative and dis-empowering.

It became very clear to me that the kind of questions I was asking myself were not enhancing the quality of my life in any way. They were leaving me feeling depressed, frustrated, and afraid. And that was not where I wanted to be.

I was asking myself "why" questions most of the time. "Why me? Why has God abandoned me and allowed this to happen to me? Why was the prostate cancer not detected before it had reached stage 4? Why has this happened at a time when my wife is so busy with her studies? Why are my children not calling often enough? Why........?"

The more "why"questions I asked myself the more dis-empowered I felt. Because they never led me to any satisfactory answer, these questions drained me of energy and left me utterly exhausted mentally, emotionally and physically. I was not loving myself. I was not being my own best friend.

As a student of personal development and a keen follower of Dr John Demartini, I clearly remembered him saying: "The quality of your life is determined by the quality of the questions you ask yourself." The "why" questions I was asking myself were certainly not enhancing the quality of my life.

I then recalled that during my training as a life coach I had learned that "why" questions should be avoided like the plague. Such questions were dis-empowering and led one to either paralysis or emotional self-defence. I had been advised to avoid asking my clients or myself questions that were prefixed by the word "why". Now facing the greatest challenge of my life, I could clearly see why "why" was not the way to go.

I also remembered learning that I should avoid asking my clients or myself questions that focused on the negative - "What do you not want?/What do I not want?" This question is dis-empowering as it gets a person to focus on what's going wrong.

My training had encouraged me to empower my clients and myself by using questions beginning with "Who.., What.., How.., When.. and Where..". Such questions would help me or my clients to self–examine, find the direction I or they needed to go and actually take action.

It must have been on the sixth day that I remembered these words from Dr John Demartini, a human behaviour specialist: "There is never a loss, only a transformation."

I thought to myself: "I certainly have 'lost' Nurse, my wife, as she is not available to me most of the day as I battle with cancer. But then where is the transformation? Who has taken her place?"

Initially these questions drew a blank. I didn't see any transformation at all. There was no one who had taken her place.

Then a light bulb switched on in my head and I saw him very clearly. He was completely available twenty-four hours a day, seven days a week and he knew more about me than any other human being. He had always been there. **He was me.** What a revelation! I was my own very best friend and would determine the quality of my journey with prostate cancer. This was a very powerful experience for me.

The moment I accepted that my wife was not in a very good space to spend much time with me was the moment of my liberation. I got to that moment after asking myself: "How much am I really there for me? What value do I really give myself? How valuable or important am I to myself? Between me and my wife who is really more responsible for my well-being?"

Not only did I free myself from living on unrealistic expectations, I also mentally and emotionally freed my wife. I let her go. She was no longer more responsible for me than I was. The buck stopped with me. I became less judgmental about what she should or should not do for me.

This shifted my mind to the realisation that I was the very first person to take care of me. I was actually more responsible for my own well-being than my wife. It was my responsibility to choose the attitudes and actions that would serve me best. That was what loving myself was all about.

It was those wake-up call questions that got me thinking. I realised that no other human being understood the emotions I was experiencing in exactly the way I was going through them. No other human being could fully empathise with the fears, frustrations, anxieties and worries I was experiencing. The only human being who understood exactly what was going on was me. Rightly, I was also the only human being who was supposed to have the highest level of interest in me.

At times, I was quite angry and frustrated with other people for not fully understanding my feelings about my situation. Then it dawned on me that they were actually doing their best, considering that they had their own lives and issues to deal with. I could never understand and appreciate their issues and challenges the way they did. So why was I expecting them to see, understand and appreciate my own situation in the same way that I did?

That got me thinking. I realised that for me to have any chance of effectively dealing with the cancer challenge that I faced, I needed two things. I needed emotional and spiritual stability. I needed clarity and connection in these two areas.

How could I emotionally help myself? Well, in the same way I could spiritually help myself. I was a Christian and I believed in God. I knew that spiritually, and even emotionally, God could help me if I developed a close relationship with him. And I had always believed that the God I talked to in my prayers lived inside me. That's when it dawned on me that I could actually help myself if I developed a close relationship with me. To be able to do that I had to go inside myself. And that was easier said than done.

The Bible I read every day told me: "Love your neighbour as yourself." What did that mean? It meant that I was my first love. It meant loving, valuing, forgiving and embracing myself first. Then it would become easier for me to love, value, forgive and embrace others. Before I could meaningfully love other people, I had to give value to and love myself. And how could I do that as I dealt with my prostate cancer challenge?

This is what it meant. While my doctor, urologist, oncologist and my wonderful wife and loving children were going to support me on my journey with this cancer, the greatest support I would ever have was going to come from me. I was going to become my number one healer and cheerleader. The attitudes that I was going to choose as I fought this challenge would determine the kind of relationship I was choosing to have with myself.

If I chose to entertain worry, doubt and self-pity and to adopt the attitude that I was a victim, I would be inviting fear, sadness, and frustrations into my life. This would inevitably lead me to becoming anxious and would eventually result in depression. There would probably be much justification for me to adopt this line of thinking. However, by choosing to be a victim, I would be behaving as my own worst enemy. That attitude would not serve me. It would sabotage the very health that I needed to nurture in myself.

My health had a better chance of restoration if I took the path of **faith**. Along this path I had to believe in the possibility of overcoming the cancer that had invaded my body. And so I chose to be my own best friend and to take a bigger role in my own healing than my family doctor, my urologist, my oncologist, naturopath, homeopath and all those medical services and personnel which were going to be involved in my treatment. I made a decision that I was not going to surrender my life to these specialists and agree to anything that they told me. I was going to do my own research, find out as much as I could about my condition and then make informed decisions. I chose to be in the forefront in my own journey with prostate cancer.

I also chose to take a bigger role than any member of my most immediate family. I was not going to make my wife or any of my five children more responsible than I was. While I recognised that they loved and cared for me, they were not responsible for my emotional states. My best attitude towards them would be to express gratitude for whatever they did for me.

Even though any one of them might not meet my expectations, whether I had a positive or negative attitude was up to me. Whether I was frowning or cheerful was my choice and total responsibility. It was not what happened out there that determined my mindset. It was how I chose to look at and respond to what happened out there. It was all about the choices I made. That was the bottom line of loving myself and being my own best friend.

I was more responsible than any of these people for making my prostate cancer experience as comfortable for me as possible. I had the first responsibility towards my own healing. Whatever attitude or response I chose to any situation, the key question I started to ask myself was: "Is this attitude or response helping my healing?" This became the rallying question that I asked myself several times a day as I confronted the greatest challenge of my life. It helped me to remain centred. It was a very powerful and highly empowering question. It constantly reminded me to love myself and to continue to remember that I was my own best friend.

I decided that if I was going to become my own number one cheerleader I would have to become more cheerful. By deciding to smile, to be positive and to take one hundred percent responsibility for my healing, I was being my own best friend and living an amazing relationship with myself.

By deciding to take full responsibility for everything that was going to happen to me I was disarming the cancer itself as well as other people and circumstances from dictating the quality of my life. I was giving myself the greatest gift possible under the circumstances that I found myself in. By deciding to make the best of each moment that I was alive, I was raising the quality of my life to levels I had never enjoyed before. I felt highly encouraged by this attitude. It helped me cope with the prostate cancer challenge in a way I had never thought possible.

It was quite liberating to no longer depend on other people completely to give me value, to tell me that I was special, valuable and lovable. After all, there hadn't been many times in my entire lifetime that people had come up to me saying: "Hey you are absolutely fantastic! I really appreciate and value who you are."

Maybe this had happened once a year for me on my birthday and on Father's Day.

I realised that all along I had been building my sense of self-worth, value, meaning and well-being on the whims, moods, feelings and judgments of other people. I had been setting myself up for failure all the time. Over the years, I had built an endless list of expectations about what I thought people should be doing for me. These expectations were just in my mind and had never been communicated to anyone. And yet they were very high and almost intense. In my mind, they were the law. That actually explained why I hardly ever felt fulfilled and almost always thought that I was not enough. Of course, no one out there could meet my unrealistic and uncommunicated expectations.

I now became aware that I had been setting myself up for failure, a lot of disappointment, anger and frustration. I awakened to the realisation that people usually don't do what we want or expect them to do for us most of the time. And how much control did I have over what other people felt, thought and behaved? It had been a fallacy and a daydream for me to expect, for well over 60 years, that people would do what I wanted them to do, in the way I wanted them to do it and at the time I wanted them to.

I was actually being challenged to love myself. I realised that the most important relationship in my life was the relationship with myself. Like every other human being, I wanted to be valued and loved. But all my life I had depended heavily on my wife and other people to give me the value and love that I needed. I had been giving my wife the first responsibility for making me feel loved.

As I looked back I realised how unwise and self-sabotaging I had been –only feeling loved because other people had decided to love me. It also meant that if I didn't feel loved, I would blame my wife and other people for not loving me. I would then hold a pity party and descend into a victim mentality. No wonder my attitude and quality of life had been in the pits most of the time.

I now realised that I could not demand that other people rise up to meet my needs at the time I expect them to and in the way that I want them to. They have their own needs to attend to first, just like my wife had her final year graduate studies to focus on. I was not necessarily her first priority. I could now see that it had been unwise, unrealistic and actually very selfish for me to expect my wife to fulfill my need to be loved and cared for.

For the very first time in my entire life, I became aware that loving and taking care of myself was my number one responsibility. Of all human beings, I was the only person who knew exactly what I wanted, the way that I wanted it and the time that I wanted it. No other person in the entire world could enter my mind, my heart, my skin and know exactly what I wanted at a particular point in my life.

I now realised how powerful my mind was. What mattered most was the attitude I chose to adopt towards myself and whatever situation I found myself in. As I faced the prostate cancer that was clearly a threat to my very life, the attitude I was going to choose was going to make all the difference. I had the power to determine the quality of my own life. I could actually use the power of my mind to motivate, encourage and inspire myself.

I felt empowered.

I also started to feel less judgmental about other people. I had been angry and upset with people before because I had not felt loved and cared for by them. I had labelled them bad people simply because they had not met my own expectations. This had been a very subjective judgement on my part. Simply because they had not met my expectation did not mean that they were bad people. They were just different from me and saw things differently. It certainly had not been fair for me to make them responsible for my own happiness and fulfillment. I now found it easier to forgive people and give them the benefit of the doubt. I was now quite happy to free them from responsibility. I also felt freed from the burden of expectations.

The greatest self-discovery I made was that when it comes to my strong desire to experience meaningful and fulfilling love, I was actually more reliable than other people. I was my number one source of the love, care and affirmation that I desire. I realised that after God, the human being I could trust more than anyone else to be truly there for me was ME.

I lived with myself twenty-four hours a day, seven days a week. I knew and experienced my desires, needs and challenges more intimately than any other person. This also meant that the answers and solutions that I would come up with in response to my needs and challenges would be the most suitable and appropriate for me.

It was refreshing and empowering for me to start experiencing how to truly and unselfishly love myself first before I could expect someone else to love me. I felt excited about the challenge of working on building an amazing relationship with myself first before I could expect to have an amazing relationship with anyone else.

It became more and more evident in my life that it was only when I gave myself genuine love, value, respect and appreciation that I began to attract genuine love, value, respect and appreciation from other people. It became clear to me that this was the law of attraction at work. What I was creating within me, I attracted from other people. How I saw myself determined how other people saw me.

I became aware of the fact that unless I appreciated who I was and gave myself the value that I deserved, no one else would. Appreciating who I was and giving myself value meant focusing on and becoming aware of my strengths. I was able to focus more on what empowered me. This became a very powerful way of motivating and inspiring myself to be the best that I could be.

Becoming my own very best friend helped me connect with my life's mission and purpose more clearly than ever before. It became very clear to me that my number one mission and purpose in life was to motivate and inspire myself and others to become the best that we could be. Knowing that I had to motivate and inspire myself first was a game-changer for me.

I began to believe more strongly that I could not give others what I didn't have myself. I had to walk my talk. Everything that I shared with other people, especially as advice, I had to live myself. Meaningful life and leadership became all about working on myself first before I could start entertaining expectations and making demands on other people.

I began to see that within my number one mission my first objective was to build an amazing relationship with myself, my God, my wife, my five children and my three grandchildren. I had to begin with myself. I could not meaningfully connect with God unless I appreciated the unconditional love and value that he gave me. I could not build meaningful relationships with my wife, children and grandchildren if I was all messed up. I could not build fruitful work, business and other social relationships if I was not able to put my own act together.

I was capable of and responsible for transforming my life more than anyone else could ever be. I had to nurture and nourish myself in every way possible. I owed it to myself.

Loving and building an amazing relationship with myself was not the same as feeding on my ego, vain pride and selfishness. It was not putting myself on a pedestal. It was not putting myself up there and thinking that I am better than someone else. As a unique person, I could not be more important than anyone else. I simply needed to embrace who I was and to give myself the value that I deserved.

I also could not be less important than anyone else. I was not loving and building a good relationship with myself by putting myself down. When I initially felt pity for myself and saw myself as a poor and helpless cancer victim, I was beating myself up and seeing myself as less important than those who did not have cancer. I was giving other people permission to look down on me. I was saying to them: "This is how I see myself – a helpless, pitiful and poor victim of prostate cancer. This is also how you should see me." I certainly grew in wisdom by realising that the world treated me the way I treated myself.

I connected with the advice I had repeatedly heard from Dr John Demartini. In most of his seminars, talks, books, DVDs and CDs he strongly advised people not to put themselves or others either down or on a pedestal. The best place to put others or yourself was in the heart just as you are. And that is where love was. I found this quite profound and empowering.

Building an amazing relationship with myself, especially as I faced prostate cancer, meant cheering myself on even when everyone else had gone quiet. It meant acknowledging, accepting and appreciating myself unconditionally. When I did all that needed to be done to encourage, motivate and inspire myself, then I would be showing true love for the special person that I was. This was treating myself as I truly deserved to be treated. This was focusing my thinking, attitude and behaviour on me - the person who mattered most in my life. If I was not thinking right, not talking right and not behaving right, I suffered and so did everybody else around me.

Giving myself love and value first significantly helped me to love and value other people as well. I became more sensitive to other people's need for love. They had as much right to be loved and valued as I had. My obligation to love and value myself began to challenge me to love and value others – unconditionally. The more my respect for other people grew, the more I respected myself.

I felt quite empowered. Not only was I able to attract loving and amazing relationships around me. I was also able to initiate and build such relationships.

Learning to love myself and to become my own best friend was by far the greatest point of personal growth arising from my encounter with prostate cancer.

It helped me to realise, appreciate and embrace that I was one hundred percent responsible for the quality of my own life. I was capable of and responsible for transforming my life more than anyone else could ever be. I deserved to nurture and nourish myself in every way possible.

Relating with myself was the only relationship where I had full control, with no other human being involved. Loving myself and being my own best friend was a choice I had to make every day.

Building an amazing relationship with myself meant forgiving myself and having the courage to say "I'm sorry" to those I knew I had offended. It meant believing that no matter what I had done or not done I was still a worthy person. I showed true love for the special person that I was when I did all that needed to be done to encourage, motivate and inspire myself.

Discovering the treasure of loving myself and being my own best friend made my journey with prostate cancer the richest experience of my entire life. The healthy, positive attitude I adopted toward myself made all the difference. It played a significant role in my fight with cancer.

The greatest testimony to that is the fact that I have been prostate cancer free for more than five years now.

Affirmations: I AM MY OWN BEST FRIEND

- *I love, value, acknowledge and appreciate myself just as I am.*
- *Every day I give myself the value, respect, love and appreciation that I deserve.*

- *I am my own best friend and talk to myself kindly every day.*
- *I am grateful for the gift that I am to myself, my family and my friends.*
- *I give top priority to building a quality relationship with myself. All other relationships come second.*
- *I focus on building and experiencing amazing relationships with myself, my God, my family and friends.*
- *I am totally responsible for ensuring that I enjoy all the love that I desire and deserve.*
- *I take 100% responsibility for the quality of life that I live every day. I am my own cheerleader and I encourage myself to go on when everyone else has gone quiet.*
- *I am my own number one hero, encourager, motivator and inspirer.*

CHAPTER 3

I EMBRACE MY BEAUTY AND MAGNIFICENCE

"You have been criticising yourself for years, and it hasn't worked. Try approving of yourself and see what happens."
Louise L. Hay

EMBRACE YOUR BEAUTY

Did you know? Where you ever aware?
Did you give your mind's eye the chance to stare?
Did you see the glitter of diamonds and pearls
That mirrored acres of the precious jewels
Lying deep inside you, beyond your eyes?

There is a beauty and magnificence deep inside
Visible to your soul, from day one fully in sight
Dancing to the beat and rhythm of your heart
Dying to show the world a rare work of art
Yearning for the embrace of your mind so unique

Will you continue to ignore the hidden treasure?
Do you not feel the weight of the burning pressure?
The readiness of the beauty and magnificence to
shine
And to be reverently embraced by your heart like a
shrine
Of abundant boundless acres of flawless diamonds

Embrace your beauty and savour the experience
Open your eyes and arms to your magnificence
See the immense depth of your priceless value
Acknowledge your source and give it value
You're born of a spirit – infinite and abundant

In your beauty and magnificence lies your mission
When you truly embrace them you'll see the vision
You'll connect with your purpose, reason and big WHY
You'll know your fears, anxieties and worries are a big lie
You'll take your rightful place and make a difference

B eing diagnosed with stage four prostate cancer initially invoked overwhelming thoughts and feelings of anger, fear, frustration and isolation. I spent the first few days feeling quite bitter and victimised. I could not imagine anything positive about myself.

Instead, I imagined this big and growing prostate cancer wound inside my body and it looked hideous and evil. I did not at all feel like a pretty sight. I did not see anything inside me that was beautiful enough for me to embrace. I felt like a thornbush.

I felt as if it was my fault that the cancer was growing inside my body. I was blaming myself and thinking that maybe if I had not been negligent or reckless with my health, I would not have been diagnosed with prostate cancer.

I became constantly worried and concerned about what people thought of me. I felt that once they knew that I had prostate cancer, they would put me in a box. I would become one of those people to be pitied and felt sorry for. My value as a living human being would start to diminish rapidly. My days in this world would be numbered.

Sooner rather than later I would be experiencing such pain that people would be pitifully wishing and praying that I got relief from the pain. They would see death as the best way out for me. I would probably be wishing the same for myself as well. I pictured the cancer monster growing bigger by the day and my poor body shrinking and becoming smaller and smaller until I was dead.

For a while I focused on and reflected on my death. Because I felt that it was more certain than ever before in my life, I somehow felt licensed to have a frank discussion with myself about it. This feeling gave me the courage to face it and openly start asking myself questions I had never asked before. How would it be like at that moment? What would I look and feel like? What thoughts would be going through my dying mind? The obvious answer that I came up with to all these questions was: "I don't know. I have no idea."

Then I asked myself a question that would soon change my attitude and outlook in a very powerful and empowering way. That question would soon define and continues to define who I am and what my life's purpose is. That question was: "How would I want to look and feel like at my point of death, at that moment when I am breathing my last?"

This time I had a very clear answer to that question: "I would want to have feelings of gratitude for the life that I had lived. I would like to feel and tell myself that I had lived a meaningful life. I would like to experience love and appreciation for the people who had come into my life. Above all I would like to feel really good about the way I had lived my life."

This led to another interesting question. "For me to feel at the end of my life that I had lived a meaningful life, what would I need to be doing between now and whenever I am going to die?"

The answer was also loud and clear: "I need to be making a positive difference in other people's lives and in the world around me."

To be able to do that I needed to shift from seeing myself as the centre of need. I needed to move away from feeling sorry for myself. I needed to move away from feeling needy and wanting people to rescue me.

I had to move towards sensitivity and awareness of other people's needs. To make a positive difference, I would have to respond to other people's needs.

My most immediate response to my cancer diagnosis had been to see myself as the person who needed help more than anyone else in the world. I had seen myself as a helpless victim who deserved pity and sympathy from myself and other people. For a while I saw myself as physically, spiritually and emotionally destitute.

However, once I started thinking about making a positive difference before I died, I began to realise that I was not the most needy person in the world. There were other people out there who were far worse off than I was and who needed help from me a lot more than I needed help from them or anyone else.

I would have to appreciate my own value to be able to make a positive difference in other people's lives. I had to convince myself that I had sufficient value and worth to be able to give to others. I could only give from my sufficiency. It was not possible to positively impact other people's lives if I thought I was unworthy. Inner emptiness could not give value to other people and make a positive difference in their lives. I had to see and embrace my own beauty and magnificence first. I had to see how abundantly blessed I was.

I had to see and appreciate how rich, beautiful and magnificent I was on the inside. Yes, this made a lot of sense to me and became the focus of my attention. Only when I saw myself in this way would I be able to impact other people's lives in a generous way.

More than anything else I had experienced since my diagnosis, this gave my life meaning and purpose. I knew immediately that I had to do something pro-actively to make that happen. I would have to have a greater appreciation of who I was and start living my life on purpose.

It was only after reflecting on and embracing the fact that I was so unique and my own best friend that my perspective of my situation began to shift. My appreciation of who I was began to grow by the day. I was not just a unique human being. The prostate cancer that I had been diagnosed with was also unique and not comparable with that which thousands of other people had been diagnosed with.

I started to connect with an inner beauty that I had never thought existed. I came face to face with a beautiful and magnificent part of me that I had never met before. It was a beauty and magnificence that was exclusive and unique to me. It was a beauty and magnificence that even the cancer could not obliterate. I began to see riches in myself that gave me an immense sense of self-value. It was more than being just special. The beauty and magnificence were just as incomparable as my unique identity.

In the midst of the biggest challenge in my entire life, I encountered God's immense love for me. This was particularly so when I fully embraced the belief that I was created in God's image. As a Christian, I remembered Psalm 139 and realised how "fearfully and wonderfully" I had been created. I thought to myself: "The creation of anything of value takes a lot of thought, love and care. There must be something beautiful in me that I was meant to decorate the world with."

The fact that I had been diagnosed with prostate cancer did not preclude the fact that I was created in the image of God and that I have a magnificence and beauty that no-one else in this whole wide world possesses. How successfully and effectively I was going to deal with this cancer was not going to be determined by whether I would die soon or after many years. It was going to be determined by the value I was going to give my life in the time remaining before my death. The more valuable a life I was going to live – long or short – the bigger a smile I would have on my face at my death. My creator endowed me with gifts and talents that I could still use to make a positive difference in the world around me.

If I could connect with and embrace the beauty, magnificence and acres of diamonds inside me, then I would be able to face the cancer with a smile on my face. I would be able to live my life with greater meaning and purpose. The more people I positively impacted with the products of my inner beauty and magnificence, the more fulfilling my life would be.

What was it that was awesome, beautiful and creative about me? What was it that I had done in my life that had given me a lot of pride? Where were the "acres of diamonds" in me?

As I reflected on the sixty odd years I had been in the world, I began to see evidence of the acres of diamonds that had always been a part of my life. I realised that, in fact, other people had seen the beauty and magnificence in me long before I did. I recalled being appointed headmaster of a big Catholic high school when I was not even a Catholic. That was only six years after I had become a teacher. They must have seen something special –some treasure and value – in me that I did not see in myself. I had not seen this myself because I had allowed a lot of critical inner voices within me to convince me that I was not that worthy.

I remembered that as headmaster I had this burning desire to motivate and inspire my students and teachers to become the best that they could be. I vividly recalled how some of my teachers had been moved by my school assembly speeches and personally told me so.

I also remembered meeting quite a few of my students many years after they had left my school. When I met them they were adults, some holding responsible jobs and others having started families. They would always tell me that they had found my assembly speeches highly motivating and inspiring, and that they had adopted and continued to use in their adult lives some of the principles and values that I had talked about.

As I recalled my days as teacher, headmaster and deputy headmaster, I realised that I must have positively impacted the lives of thousands of students and hundreds of the teachers that I had worked with. It was only now – after I had been diagnosed with prostate cancer – that I was, for the very first time, appreciating the fact that I had made a big positive difference in the lives of so many people.

After I had left the world of formal teaching and running schools, I became a personal development consultant with a focus on working with teenagers and young adults. Within five years I had played a significant role in motivating and inspiring almost a thousand teenagers and young adults to become the best that they could be. Through the medium of a highly transformational programme I helped young people become more focused, goal directed, self-confident and self-motivated.

While I was running schools, and involved with personal development, I was also making a positive difference working as a volunteer. My wife and I spent a significant amount of our time after hours and on weekends counselling HIV/AIDS patients in hospitals in Harare, Zimbabwe.

From 1981 to 2005 my wife and I had been volunteers involved in running marriage workshops for a worldwide Catholic organisation. Besides our own personal growth as a couple we had positively impacted the relationships of hundreds of married couples.

I had actually felt quite fulfilled doing voluntary work. It gave my life a lot of meaning and purpose. I certainly enjoyed doing it.

Even at the time of my diagnosis in Sydney Australia, I was also making a positive difference as a volunteer for an immigrant services organisation. My wife and I were working with another Catholic organisation and were involved in visiting Catholic parishes on Saturdays and Sundays, giving talks and raising funds to help disadvantaged communities throughout the world.

Reflecting on all these activities helped me realise and appreciate that I had an incredible amount of value. I had acres of diamonds within. I was beautiful inside. I had the gift of motivating and inspiring other people to become the best that they could be. I also enjoyed doing voluntary work and making a positive difference in other people's lives. I just had not embraced and appreciated my beauty and magnificence before. But now I could feel it. I could touch it. I had immense value!

I became acutely aware that the beauty, magnificence and leader in me were not there just to decorate my life. I was like a tree planted by God in this world, and beauty, magnificence and the leader in me were the flowers on the tree. The flowers and the tree existed not just to decorate the world, but more importantly to bear fruit and to give life to the world. My inner beauty and magnificence felt like a light shining so intensely inside me that I could not contain it. I had to open my heart and let that light go out and positively impact other people's lives. My beauty and magnificence had a purpose – to impact the world in a way that only I could. The imprint of that impact would make an impression that was only as uniquely beautiful and magnificent as I was.

I recalled this famous poem "Our deepest fear" from Marriane Williamson

Our deepest fear is not that we are inadequate.
Our deepest fear is that we are powerful beyond measure.
It is our light, not our darkness
That most frightens us.

We ask ourselves
Who am I to be brilliant, gorgeous, talented, fabulous?
Actually, who are you not to be?
You are a child of God.

Your playing small
Does not serve the world.
There's nothing enlightened about shrinking
So that other people won't feel insecure around you.

We are all meant to shine,
As children do.
We were born to make manifest
The glory of God that is within us.
It's not just in some of us;
It's in everyone.

And as we let our own light shine,
We unconsciously give other people permission to do
the same.
As we're liberated from our own fear,
Our presence automatically liberates others

From 1994 to 2006 I had this poem displayed on the built-in cupboard in the master bedroom of our house. For 12 years I had read those powerful words almost every day and they had become etched in my mind.

And now as I reflected on my inner beauty and magnificence, in March 2011 just after the prostate cancer diagnosis, the power of the quotation flooded both my heart and mind.

For the first time ever in my 63 years in this world I became aware that I had been afraid to face the true value of who I really was. It took a prostate cancer diagnosis to enable me to see and begin to appreciate the 'light' that was in me.

Far from seeing myself as a victim, my self-image was lifted up to levels I had never thought possible. Yes I was "powerful beyond measure". In spite of the diagnosis I had the capacity to make a positive difference in the world around me. After all it was just a diagnosis. I was not feeling any pain. I was not ill. Actually I was physically feeling well. All I needed to do was focus on my wellness. I could use that wellness as a source of power in me. I could use this power not only to help me fight the cancer that was growing inside my body, but also to make a greater positive difference in the world around me than I had ever done before.

My initial response to the prostate cancer diagnosis was virtually giving up on life. I did not believe that I stood a chance. I was ready to give death the benefit of the doubt. I was asking myself 'Who am I to stand up against prostate cancer?'

But now as I reflected on Marriane Williamson's words I felt empowered and emboldened. Who was I not "to be brilliant, gorgeous, talented, fabulous?" I was "a child of God." I was meant "to make manifest the glory of God that is within" me. And there was no better way to do it than focusing on making a positive difference in the world around me.

My playing small as a victim of cancer did not serve me or anyone else. There was "nothing enlightened about shrinking" in the face of the cancer that threatened my life. I was 'meant to shine' in spite of it.

I felt inspired to share my story with the world. I felt compelled to share my mental journey with cancer. In doing so I would be letting my "own light shine" and hopefully in the process I would be giving "other people permission to do the same."

By sharing my journey with cancer in a positive light I believed I would be liberating myself from "my own fear". My genuine hope was that this gesture "automatically liberates others." After all I was convinced that all of us had the capacity to face our "greatest fears" with a positive mindset.

"It's not just in some of us; it's in everyone."

Reflecting on Marriane Williamson's poem helped me to realise that my inner beauty and magnificence manifested themselves in my ability to motivate and inspire myself and others, especially young people, to become the best that we could be. It was very clear to me that my challenge was to motivate and inspire myself first as I faced prostate cancer.

To be aware of and acknowledge my unique identity was only the first step on my self-awareness journey. In order to completely embrace who I was, I could now go deeper and bring out my inner beauty and magnificence. And then I could embrace it and put it to work.

Facing prostate cancer and seeing my beauty and magnificence at the same time made me want so much to live. I had so much to give and I wasn't going to be able to do that if I died. I wanted so much to give more and so I wanted to live more.

My beauty and magnificence was a reason to live and I had acres of diamonds inside me that the world had not yet seen. I had very positive reasons to live and I prayed for life and health. I got life and health. I am still here today as I share my story with you.

My experience convinced me that there is a beauty and magnificence that resides in each and every one of us. This beauty and magnificence contains the seeds of who we are really meant to be. When you come face to face with your beauty and magnificence your life will never be the same again. It is a paradigm shift. You realise what a beautiful and wonderful creation of God you are. You also realise that your beauty and magnificence have always been there right from the beginning

What had prevented me from recognising my beauty and magnificence for many years were the gremlins that lived inside me and that dominated my thinking. As I grew up and experienced different situations and events, I acquired certain critical inner voices that told me that I was not worth much, couldn't do it or I was incapable. Other people's comments or attitudes towards me could have given birth to these gremlins. It certainly was also a result of my own self-doubt. The overall result was that I had operated on a paradigm dominated by thoughts of self-limitation. For many years my self-image, self-belief and self-confidence became permanently paralysed.

It took me an encounter with prostate cancer to see my real value. Only when I felt that my life was being taken away, did I realise how rich I was and indeed how much richer I could be. This gave me a lot of reasons to want to go on living. I was too valuable to die.

Another realisation I had was that for many years I had developed a negative self-talk. Over and over again I had heard this voice emphatically speaking into my life, "You are not worthy of success! You were never meant to succeed in this life. You will never make it! You are a victim of circumstances. Life is too difficult. Who do you think you are?"

I had repeatedly put myself down with those negative words I subconsciously and regularly said to myself. Those words became a major stumbling block whenever I tried to move forward in my life. The more negative my self-talk, the less able I was to see, appreciate and embrace my beauty and magnificence.

I also realised that many times I had justified thinking and saying negative things to myself. When things were not going well for me or I had messed up, I felt justified to condemn myself. I saw that as confirmation that I was not good enough. I was unforgiving of myself. I was quick to believe that I was a bad person and was always going to be a bad person. With such a negative paradigm and mindset, how could I ever see and embrace my own beauty and magnificence?

It was only when I came face to face with my own death that I realised how self-damning and damaging my negative self-talk had been. For the first time in my entire life I began to understand and appreciate that the quality of my self-talk determined how I felt about myself and ultimately the quality of my life. Only positive self-talk was going to help me grow and become more aware of my own inner beauty and magnificence. Only positive self-talk was going to help me fight the cancer I faced with any chance of success.

As a result, I decided to shift my paradigm and replace my subconscious negative self-talk with positive self-talk or affirmations. Throughout my eighteen months of cancer treatment I had a growing list of positive statements that I said to myself everyday.

Today I have more than thirty affirmations that I say to myself almost daily. That has made a big positive difference in my life and has empowered me to embrace my own beauty and magnificence.

I could now take full responsibility for keeping myself aware of my inherent value daily. No other human being could motivate and inspire me to the full extent of my own deepest desires. Even if I was to tell them how I wanted to be motivated and inspired, they would never fully grasp what I was talking about. And much as they might try to motivate and inspire me, they would never do it to my full satisfaction. My expectations would be disappointed.

I became aware that I was the only person who could measure up to the standards that met my deepest desires.

In spite of my human imperfections, I had an inherent value that only I could most meaningfully connect with. No one else could completely see and fully experience it as much as I did. No one could appreciate and express as deep a gratitude for it as I could. And no one else could affirm me more effectively than myself.

Until I got in touch with the immense value, the inner beauty and magnificence that resides within me, I could not fully appreciate how awesome I was and the enormous power that I had to achieve much more than ever before in my entire life. This connection empowered and enabled me to fully grasp the potential and range of possibilities that lay in my path.

The less I compared myself with others, the more of my beauty and magnificence I saw. One of the most powerful truths I have ever come across is the universal law that states: "What you focus on expands". Over the years whenever I have focused on other people, especially on how much better they were than me. The more superior they appeared to me, the more inferior I felt.

It was only when I began to deliberately focus on my own beauty and magnificence that I began to see more and more evidence of them. I was not necessarily seeing myself as better than other people. It was more of an appreciation of my own unique value and worth which no one else possessed in the way that I did. It was a powerful mind shift for me.

Recognising my own areas of giftedness was another step in the process of embracing my own magnificence. What could I do best and feel unbridled in the process of doing it? When I got in touch with my own creativity I would be getting very close to embracing my magnificence. When I experienced gratitude for my gifts and talents, it meant that I was in touch with my magnificence. I increasingly began to feel tears of gratitude coming to my eyes whenever I made an inner and detailed connection with the gifts, talents and blessings that I started to see in my life.

I also found that embracing my own magnificence meant that while recognising that I was not perfect, I didn't need to focus on my faults. Instead, as I faced the scourge of cancer, I felt encouraged to spend most of my time focused on my value, on the many gifts, talents and abilities that I possessed.

What this meant was that I was focusing on the best in me at that point in time. And it didn't matter how bad I might have thought I was. There was still something wonderfully special about me at each moment if I cared enough to look for it. And whenever I seriously focused on the good in me and I looked for it, I would always find it. At first it was difficult and took a lot of concentrated effort. But with repeated practice it became easier and easier to see the best in me.

My cancer experience was an amazing training ground for me to learn to embrace the beauty and magnificence in me. When I started seeing and appreciating the value I had, I felt empowered to visualise the best that I could become – a person free of cancer. I began to see possibilities of how different my life could be. This enabled me to empower myself to bring out the very best that I could be and to make a positive difference in my own life and in the world around me.

Once I could vividly imagine and visualise myself free of cancer, I became energised to go for it and do everything I could to make it happen. With the passing of each day of the eighteen months of my treatment I grew in belief and confidence that it was possible to become cancer-free once again.

I have been cancer-free for more than six years now. I continue to find immense and transformational benefits in embracing my own beauty and magnificence. This attitude has transformed my life. It has enabled me to face and overcome all the fears that stand between where I am now and the very best I believe I can become.

I sincerely believe that your life will also be positively different if you decide to embrace your own beauty and magnificence. You will come face to face with the endless depth of your own value. You will discover the sprawling "acres of diamonds" that lie within you. You will significantly raise your levels of self-belief and self-confidence.

As you embrace your beauty and magnificence, you will begin to appreciate that you are complete just as you are. This enables you to release the inherent powers and energies that lie within. You empower and energise yourself for higher levels of creativity, performance and achievement. You enter the stimulating world of possibility thinking and continuously raise the bar for yourself so that you are able to maximise your potential.

You become your own best friend, are much kinder to yourself. You become your number one leader, encourager, motivator and inspirer. You also become your number one hero. You are able to forgive yourself more easily while at the same time challenging yourself to higher levels of who you can be and what you can do.

You experience a significant growth in your relationships – with your creator, with your family and other people that you closely interact with. You connect with other people's beauty and magnificence too and you help them see their own beauty and magnificence. Together you are able to maximise your impact and to create a synergy that transforms the world around you.

You begin to accept other people as they are and for who they are. It becomes easier to forgive them as their magnificence and beauty overshadows their imperfect characters and behaviours.

You realise that together you maximise your impact in making a positive difference in the world around you. By embracing your own magnificence and beauty you light and ignite other people's lives so that they also begin to see how magnificently created they are.

You are able to separate your self-worth from your performance. You realise that your true worth is not determined by the score sheet of your performance but by an inherent underlying value which you do not earn but simply have. You are able to separate what you have done from who you are.

You become empowered to confirm your uniquely incomparable identity and realise that the authenticity of your magnificence and beauty lies in this identity that no one else has ever had or will ever have. The less you compare yourself with others, the more of your own magnificence and beauty you will see.

When you embrace your own beauty and magnificence, you possess the potential to enjoy the best mental and physical health possible. Now that you have a greater appreciation of your own value, you more consciously make every effort to take care of the special person that you are.

Above all, you are able to connect with the bigger vision of your mission and purpose in life and to give yourself the power to be the best that you can be.

Affirmations: I EMBRACE MY BEAUTY AND MAGNIFICENCE

- *I have an inner beauty and magnificence that is exclusive and unique to me.*
- *There are acres of diamonds within me and with which I am meant to decorate the world.*
- *I possess a beauty and magnificence that no challenge on earth can obliterate.*
- *I am a creation of immense value and I am 'fearfully and wonderfully made.' (Psalm 139)*

- *I connect with and embrace my own beauty and magnificence and I feel empowered to overcome the challenges I face.*
- *I use my inner beauty and magnificence to make a positive difference in other people's lives.*
- *I forgive myself and this enables me to see my own beauty and magnificence more clearly.*
- *I talk more positively and kindly to myself and this connects me with my beauty and magnificence.*
- *I am in touch with the immense value, inner beauty and magnificence that I possess and this makes me feel awesome.*
- *I embrace my own beauty and magnificence by recognising the gifts and talents that I have.*
- *I am raising my levels of self belief and self-confidence by embracing my own beauty and magnificence.*
- *I embrace my inner beauty and magnificence and this enables me to connect with the bigger vision of my mission and purpose in life.*

CHAPTER 4

I HAVE A PURPOSE

*"Efforts and courage are not enough
without purpose and direction."*
John F. Kennedy

PURPOSE

This life can only be lived in the present
You cannot duplicate your presence
It is a special gift that is unrepeatable
It will only make sense if you're capable
Of journeying through life with a purpose.

With an identity no one else possesses
And a value only your creator embraces
Your purpose is unique to who you are
Only understood by the mind you wear
A child of your one and only imagination

It began with the decision of your birth
Why you were gifted with life and breath
Your arrival - the manifestation of a vision
Your creation into existence with a mission
You're here to make a unique impression

Making a positive difference – that's purpose
Fulfilling your life and filling full other people's
Recognising your gifts possessed by no other
Responding to the needs of sister and brother
Changing lives, reaching goals, inspiring dreams

When it's worthy and you connect with meaning
And you would rather be thriving than leaving
When thoughts and actions are sources of energy
And mastermind liaisons become sources of synergy
You fully embrace life and truly live with purpose

Giving meaning to my life and being clear about the purpose of my existence turned my journey with cancer into a period of tremendous growth.

For many years I had waffled my way through life without a clear focus of where I was going and what I should seriously be doing with my life. I had some dreams and goals written down but I wasn't seriously connected to them and I attached little or no urgency in pursuing my dreams.

I believed I had all the time in the world. And so I was just drifting. Being diagnosed with prostate cancer was a wake-up call and brought a loud and clear message. Death was real. Death was here. I could die at any time. What if this was my time to go, to say goodbye to the world? How would I feel as I breathed my last? Would I be happy with myself? Would I say to myself I had done the best I could with everything I had? Would I have a smile on my face?

I would definitely not be happy with myself. I would not say that I had done my best with everything I had. I had not fully lived my life with purpose and meaning. I felt a huge gap between where I was and where I wanted to be. There certainly would have been no smile on my face if I had faced my death at that point. I did not feel fulfilled. I had quite a few regrets. Although I had positively impacted the lives of quite a few people, I did not think I had done enough, especially when I considered how gifted I believed I was. I also had regrets about the many opportunities to make a difference and to grow that I felt I had failed to use.

I knew that the more regrets I had, the less likelihood that there would be a smile on my face, whether I was at my point of death or not. I also knew that the more grateful I was about what I had done or had received in my life the more positively disposed I would be and the more chances there would be to have a smile on my face. As it was at that moment in my life I had more regrets than reasons to be grateful. I was convinced that finding and fully living my purpose would reduce my regrets. And because my life was under the greatest threat ever, it was more urgent than ever before that I should start reversing the ratio of my regrets to things I felt grateful for.

This jolted me into action like never before. I had to quickly clarify my life's purpose. It became crystal clear to me that it was having a purpose that would give my life true meaning. Whether I was going to live a short or long life, what was I going to meaningfully fill my days with? What was it that I could do that would give me a feeling of fulfillment and a smile on my face as I breathed my last? It was clearly urgent that I come up with some clear and meaningful answers.

Then it dawned on me that if I was to have any chances of successfully fighting the cancer that had invaded my body I had to see meaning and purpose in my life. The less value I saw in my life, the less chances I had of defeating the cancer. Meaning and purpose was a source of energy, willpower the resolve to prevail in the face of cancer or any other challenge for that matter. I was more likely to give up if I saw no meaning and purpose in my life.

The vision of a "smile on my face "as I breathed my last became and still is an obsession with me. It has become a constant reminder for me to do the very best I can in living out what I believe is my life's purpose. I often look at myself smiling in the mirror so as not to lose sight of the facial expression that I want to be my final physical farewell to the world. I have often thought of it as "a smile that gives life to death". That smile on my face truly connects me with my purpose. It gives so much meaning to my life.

Once I became aware of how unique I was, it also helped me realize and appreciate that my mission and purpose in this world was as unique as I was. I had a value that no one else possessed. My purpose could never be exactly the same as someone else's. It might be in the same area or field as many other people, but the way it manifests itself and the details of its execution were unique to me.

My unique purpose was meant to have a unique impact in the world. If I did not live to the full what I saw as my purpose, I would be depriving the world of a uniquely positive impact that no one else could make in exactly the same way that I could. I would be failing my legacy. I would be creating a gap that no one else could fill. Realising that my purpose was as unique as I was helped me appreciate that I truly mattered in this world. For the first time in 63 years I became aware that I could create a lot more meaning in my life by clarifying and working on my unique purpose.

Living my purpose to the full was a great responsibility that I could not delegate to anyone else. I felt challenged. Delegating my purpose would be like cloning myself, making myself someone's copycat or making them my copycat. As a unique individual, I did not have to imitate or be a copycat to someone else. That realisation brought about a freedom and energy that were quite inspirational for me. I felt unapologetic and complete to be who I was just as I was. I didn't have to change myself to fit into someone else's mould. This gave me a refreshing energy to want to live.

This was highly empowering and inspiring to me. I didn't have to be anyone's copy. I could be anything I chose to be as long as I was bold enough to be me. I didn't have to be like anyone else. My purpose and what I did with my life didn't have to be an imitation of anyone else. It could be something that no one else had ever done before. I didn't need to get anyone's approval. I was unique.

The key thing for me was to believe in my unique identity, get in touch with my unique purpose and then experience the joy of fulfilling that purpose.

By December 2011 I had settled into a comfortable job in Australia. I was doing pretty well in this job and was actually enjoying it. I was guaranteed to keep this job for the rest of my working life. In fact, it was my first permanent job since coming to Australia in February 2006. I was working for a non-governmental charity organisation and I was experiencing some fulfillment from working with children and families from the economically disadvantaged sector of the Sydney community.

However, I did not feel at home in that career. I was still unfulfilled and convinced that I was not really living my life's mission and purpose. There was clearly something more to life than that secure job that I had. Yes, the job certainly gave me financial security but it clearly was not the answer to my search for meaning in life. I was not doing what I truly and passionately loved to do.

I was extremely fortunate as an immigrant to have the secure job that I had. However, despite having this very good job I still felt restless. I felt incomplete.

For me purpose was something that inspired me to embrace life with enthusiasm. I saw living with purpose as engaging in activities that not only fulfilled me but also made a positive difference in the world around me. It was all about doing what I love, loving what I do and at the same time touching other people's lives. I certainly was making a positive difference in people's lives with my job.

I also happened to have got that job just after the cancer diagnosis. And so it provided much needed financial security as I faced a long and financially demanding cancer treatment programme. I told my new employers about my diagnosis and they gave me a lot of support and encouragement that I still appreciate to this day, more than six years later.

However, I didn't quite feel at home in that job. I felt restless and kept telling myself: "This is not what my life is meant to be all about. I am here for something different to this. I don't feel sincerely connected to this job. This does not feel like a part of my dream, purpose and mission in this world. If I do not connect with my true mission and purpose I will not live a fulfilling and meaningful life. I will also have less chances of surviving the cancer. It is now more important than ever before that I clarify, connect with and urgently pursue my mission and purpose. There is no time to waste!"

Since coming to Australia, I was increasingly growing in the conviction that my number one purpose was to be a teacher of love and wisdom. I was in the world to motivate and inspire myself and others to be the best that we can be. My life's mission was to embrace the magnificence and beauty that my creator planted in me and then inspire other people to do the same. I saw myself fulfilling this purpose as a writer, coach, speaker and philanthropist. And since February 2014 I have additionally seen myself doing this as a songwriter. Whenever I imagined myself motivating and inspiring myself and others (especially young people) to become the best that we can be, I felt totally fulfilled. This was the legacy I wanted to leave behind.

I loved writing. Throughout my entire adult life, I have always loved and I still love to capture in writing any thoughts and ideas that I felt were important. For more than 40 years I have developed the habit of always carrying a notebook and a pen with me wherever I go and ensuring that I captured moments of inspiration and everything of significance that happened in my life. I also kept an exercise book at home where I captured thoughts, ideas and inspirations. And since becoming computer literate, I have increasingly used my laptop for the same purpose.

I always pictured myself writing a book about my life's experiences and also about the wisdom that I believed I had accumulated over the years. I was convinced that there were people out there who would benefit from my experiences and ideas and writing was one of the important ways of communicating with them.

I also had a growing conviction that one of the best ways to leave a legacy behind for my children, grandchildren and great grandchildren was in writing. I did not know much about my own father and mother as well as my grandparents on both sides of my parentage. The little that I knew was from hearsay and was probably less than half the truth of who they really were. Many times, I have wished and continue to wish often that my parents and grandparents had left the stories of their lives in writing. But then my parents were not literate enough to have written the stories of their lives. And my grandparents and great-grandparents could not read or write. I am fully literate and have no excuse at all to deprive my children, grandchildren and great-grandchildren from knowing about my life.

The prostate cancer diagnosis disrupted that vision and almost wiped it off the canvas of my imagination. The most immediate and compelling message it communicated was that my life had come to an end and there was no reason to live. At first the diagnosis seemed to be clearly saying to me: "Pack up your dreams and throw them away! It's time to die!"

My prostate cancer diagnosis became my wake-up call in this regard. I strongly felt that my children, grandchildren and great-grandchildren had a right to know who I was and what my thoughts, ideas and values were. It was my responsibility to ensure that this information was available for them. Writing was my most effective way of communicating with the present and the future. And so I decided that I was going to be a writer. If I became a bestselling author in the process that would be a bonus. The far more important outcome for me was that I would be leaving behind a legacy that would touch the lives of my lineage for decades if not centuries after my death.

I also saw writing as the fueling foundation of my deep desire to motivate and inspire people, especially youth, to become the best that they can be. I knew I was capable of creating, through writing, motivational and inspirational programmes. Back in 2004 I had actually created and tested a programme that I called *Building Success Attitudes (BSA)*. That programme has now been revised and renamed *Creating Success Attitudes (CSA)*. I visualised myself creating more programmes that would positively impact other people's lives.

Up to the time of my prostate cancer diagnosis, writing had been a dream that was out there in the sky and for which I had done very little. The diagnosis became a wake-up call and moment of truth for me. I could no longer afford to continue to procrastinate. There was no time to waste. Time was of the essence. Death became a real possibility and that possibility became a very strong motivation for me to act. In fact, my experience with cancer became the most topical and relevant subject to base my first book on. There was no better subject to start writing about. I could start documenting my experiences almost immediately. I felt inspired to write.

I took my writing more seriously than I had ever done before. I felt more passionate about it than I had ever done before. I had a deep yearning and desire to live for many more years so that I could touch many people's lives and make a positive difference in the world through my writing.

I had realised even at the time of my diagnosis that my cancer experience would provide me with material to write my very first book. I began to pray that I would live long enough to write that book. I am so happy and grateful now that I have been given the opportunity to do so.

And so the cancer diagnosis awakened me to re-commit to use writing as a vehicle to fulfill my life's mission and purpose – to motivate and inspire thousands of people to become the best that they can be and to live fulfilling lives. My vision, dream and commitment to becoming a bestselling author continues to grow. Starting with this book I have already imagined, conceived and given title to three other books.

Before the prostate cancer diagnosis, I had been a teacher and school administrator for a total of 30 years. That experience had left a very strong impression on my mind about the power and influence of speech. And so as I now reflected on how I was going to fulfill my life's mission and purpose – to motivate and inspire thousands of people to become the best that they can be – I felt very strongly attracted to pursue public speaking as a career.

When I was growing up I didn't want, at all, to be a teacher. However, circumstances had dragged me, screaming and kicking, right to the front of the classroom.

I hated public speaking with a passion. Throughout my school days I was absolutely terrified of standing in front of a group of people and speaking. On two occasions, I had literally frozen when asked to speak to a group of my peers. I stood there, opened my mouth and nothing came out. At that time, I totally agreed with the observation that public speaking was the number one fear worldwide, ahead of the fear of death.

At the time that I completed my high school education, I was sure that I was going to be studying for a degree in economics at university. However, by the time I went to university I had been shocked into the conviction that I had to do a teaching degree. That was what would guarantee me a job after my university studies. As a black person, an economics degree would be a guarantee for unemployment. And so I became a teacher.

Reluctantly I learnt how to speak to my students in the classroom environment. In the process, I discovered that standing in front of a class and teaching them something they didn't know before was a very highly empowering tool. It certainly gave me authority, but more importantly it gave me the power to influence young minds. I discovered that I actually enjoyed positively influencing young people and that teaching them was the best way of doing so.

After my first six years as a teacher I was appointed headmaster of a boarding high school of more than 800 boys and girls. From speaking in front of my classes of students I was now speaking to the whole school including teachers. I also had opportunities to speak to my students' parents. Through my speeches as teacher and headmaster, I discovered that I could wield tremendous influence. I discovered that I had the capacity to inspire people through the spoken word. Although I was never completely comfortable as a speaker, most of the fear I used to have was gone. I developed a very high level of respect for public speaking.

And so, as I reflected on my life's purpose after my prostate cancer diagnosis, I decided that public speaking was going to be one of the ways I was going to motivate and inspire people to become the best that they could be. I became convinced that it was one of the most effective ways of communicating with large groups of people. Speaking one on many was going to be one of the ways I was going to use to fulfill my life's purpose.

In addition to writing and speaking, I also strongly felt that I could inspire people to become the best that they could be as a life coach. This inclination was inspired by several experiences that I had gone through.

During my experience as a teacher and school administrator I had many people coming to me for advice. They brought their challenges to me with a high expectation that I would help them and in most cases I did. These people included students and teachers. Occasionally I would also get parents bringing their problems to my attention and expecting me to help them with advice which I did.

While I was teaching and running schools, my wife and I started working with married couples on a voluntary basis. We were involved in a leadership role – organising and facilitating weekend marriage communication workshops. During these workshops, we would give presentations in which we would mostly share about our own relationship. In the process of doing this we would help the participating married couples to work on improving their own relationships. During the weekend–long workshops, couples would also come to us with their relationship challenges. In many cases we were able to help them. In addition to this, we also got involved in running marriage preparation sessions for engaged couples and also for couples who had been living together but now wanted to get married formally.

My wife and I obtained a counseling qualification and got involved in counseling HIV/AIDS patients in hospitals. We were doing this on a voluntary basis and we found our counseling sessions quite fulfilling. It was very clear that our counseling clients were benefitting immensely from our engagement with them.

At the beginning of the 21st Century I left my formal teaching and school administration work and went into business. In 2001, I acquired a franchise from an international personal and leadership development organisation. I started to market and facilitate personal and leadership development programmes offered by this organisation. Inspired by my high school teaching experience I focused on a programme for teenagers and young adults. Within a few years I witnessed the positive transformation of the lives of almost a thousand teenagers and young adults who were exposed to this programme. The fulfillment I experienced here convinced me that I could also facilitate the personal development of individuals through coaching.

I was so convinced that I was cut out to be a coach that in 2009 I obtained a coaching qualification from an Australian coaching institute.

Fulfilling my life's purpose as a writer, speaker and coach became an obsession and a driving force behind my prayers. As a Christian, I had always had room for prayer in my life. I had some faith in God and believed that he answers my prayers. I also knew that God's answer to my prayers was not always going to be exactly in line with my expectations.

By the time I was diagnosed with prostate cancer I had also developed a highly fulfilling habit of engaging in charitable voluntary activities. Besides working with married and engaged couples as well as HIV/AIDS patients, I also enjoyed working with young people from disadvantaged backgrounds. Helping such young people develop positive mindsets and overcome the challenges of their social environment became something I was quite passionate about. This gave my life a lot of meaning and purpose.

And so, as I faced the greatest challenge of my life, I resolved that I was going to give my life meaning and purpose by motivating and inspiring people to be the best they could be. I decided that I was going to do that as a writer, speaker, coach and charity worker

By the sixth day after my cancer diagnosis, I had a new realisation. It was a new awareness that was directly influenced by my cancer situation. It was the importance of motivating and inspiring myself first. Making a positive difference in my own life through loving myself and embracing my own magnificence became my primary purpose. Unless I took good care of myself and worked hard to claim back my health, I would be in no position to help other people. It certainly was a very empowering paradigm shift for me. It might sound selfish and inward looking but it made and still makes a lot of sense to me. Even today it is still part of my purpose, to motivate and inspire myself first so that I become empowered to motivate and inspire other people. I see it as a very important aspect of walking my talk. It is a very important part of my life's purpose.

The cancer experience connected me to the urgency of my mission and vision and gave me a commitment to it that I had never had before. Since then I have felt driven by a voice that continually tells me that there is no time to waste. It whispers urgently to me: "Remember you almost lost your life. You don't know whether it will be taken away tomorrow or next week or next year. Do what you have to do now. Live your life with purpose. There is no time to waste! You have to do something daily and consistently that makes a positive difference in other people's lives."

The powerful realisation I had was that whether my life in this world was going to be long or short, I had to give it a lot more meaning and purpose than I had ever done before. The more often I would be able to say: "It's good to be alive", the more meaningful my life would be This could only happen if I was making a positive difference in other people's lives.

I also became more aware of the power of the moment. Was I meaningfully living my 'now' moment? Was I being present? It was not about yesterday or tomorrow. It was all about now! It was not about feeling guilty and having regrets about yesterday. It was not about having fears, worries and anxieties about tomorrow. It was all about focusing on and utilising the positive and empowering energies of the 'now moment'.

I came face to face with what it means to live my life to the full. I realised that it means not fooling around. It means filling every moment with either an action or a thought that makes me feel fully alive and will have the impact of making a positive difference in the world around me. This includes a smile, a laugh, a hug or a compliment. It also includes inspiring thoughts of wisdom, creativity or inspiration.

Living life to the full means having the courage to do all those things I had always known were great things but had been afraid to do them. It is stepping right into the thick of the world I used to be scared of and getting fully involved with it. It is shifting my thinking from focusing on life's impossibilities to focusing on a world colourfully filled with possibilities.

To know what to do each and every day of the very short life that I realised I had, I had to be absolutely clear about my purpose. Otherwise I would spend this short and very valuable life experimenting, trying this and that and the other. My life would be an utter waste.

I recalled these powerful words from Dr Myles Munroe: "The greatest tragedy is not death. The greatest tragedy is life without a purpose." To have life and health and then waste them in a purposeless and directionless existence would certainly be a tragedy. I had no intention of making my life an experiment. I had to be absolutely clear about what I wanted.

Instead of focusing on my possible death from cancer, I chose to focus on putting meaning and purpose to the time space that I had between wherever I was and my death, whenever it was going to be.

After all, my death would just be a moment, maybe just a few seconds, when I would breathe my last and my physical body would become lifeless. Whenever it was going to come, my moment of death would have no value. I could not put value to death. The only value I could give my death was dignity – dying with dignity. And that dignity could only come from having lived my life with a purpose.

I certainly could not control my death but I could always put value to the time before my death. And the only part of that time which I could control was the present moment. While I could not influence my death, I certainly had the power to influence the kind of life I wanted to live.

I could put value on the life that I lived before my death, whether that life was short or long. I could choose whether or not to give my life meaning and purpose. The more meaning and purpose I gave my life, the more value it would have.

I felt challenged to give much greater value than ever before to the opportunity to be alive that was before me. As I reflected more on the meaning of life I began to appreciate more than ever before how precious it was to be alive. For all the years that I had lived I had not appreciated how much of a special gift this life was. I realised that it was not so much the length of the time that I lived in this world, but rather its quality – how I chose to live that life.

Before I was diagnosed with prostate cancer I used to have the luxury of thinking that I had plenty of time. I had a tendency of not facing my life and doing what needed to be done with any sense of urgency. I used to procrastinate a lot and use such excuses as: "I can't because I don't have the ability to do it."

It took me knowing that I had an aggressive form of prostate cancer to realise that I already had everything that it took to live out my 'short' life's purpose. I had the ability and I had the resources. I had always possessed everything I needed to be who I was meant to be. It was all up to me to connect with my life's purpose and to be the best that I was meant to be.

Affirmation   I HAVE A PURPOSE

- *I live and breathe for a purpose that is unique to me .*
- *What I can do no one else can do in exactly the same way I can do it.*

- *I am making a unique impact in the world as I live my unique purpose.*
- *I am living my purpose by doing what I love and loving what I do*
- *I feel inspired to fully use my gifts and talents with excitement and enthusiasm.*
- *I am living my purpose and making a positive difference in the world around me.*
- *I feel empowered to face challenges as I live my life with meaning and purpose.*
- *Mine is the only approval I need to choose and to live my life's purpose.*
- *I fully believe in the great value of the purpose I have embraced for my life*
- *I have a clear vision and mission and this gives my life true meaning and purpose.*

CHAPTER 5

I HAVE POTENTIAL

"You can be anything you want to be, if you only believe with sufficient conviction and act in accordance with your faith; for whatever the mind can conceive and believe, it can achieve."
Napoleon Hill

With wild mind pictures it all seems possible
Imagination runs wild and nothing's imposssible
High in the sky your thoughts have no boundaries
It all seems so real in your big mind's factories
So much fun and joy in your make-believe world

What a big spoilsport this thing called reality
Stripping my mind and dreams of their quality
Telling me "Stop dreaming and be realistic!
Why waste time building a world that's plastic.
You're too small, day dreaming and unrealistic."

You feel inadequate and don't even measure up
To your daily challenges that rear their heads up
So insurmountable, confirming your inadequacy
In ever living up to your dreams with any accuracy
And so you 'come to your senses' and stop dreaming

But there's really no peace when you stop dreaming
With restless unease the images keep swimming
You were born of the creator, you're born to create
Co-creator, connect with your source just start to create
You already have here and now everything you need

To think you can or to think you can't it is your choice
Speak your dreams into creation – use your voice
Reject "I can't!" You've opened many cans of "can'ts"
Believe, embrace - "I can!" and open your can of "cans"
You have potential, just maximise it, it is unlimited!

Embrace your full potential, go all the way uninhibited
Believe in your full potential to sow to heights unlimited
Use your full potential you cannot possibly exhaust it
Realise your full potential, it is your duty to boost it
Choose who you want to be and become your destiny

When you have the luxury of thinking that you have plenty of time, there is a tendency not to face your life and do what needs to be done with any sense of urgency.

You tend to procrastinate and use such excuses as: "I can't because I don't have the ability to do it. I am not as gifted as Jim is. I don't have the time." You find time to get busy doing other things which are of little significance. That which is important keeps on getting rescheduled.

In the midst of my prostate cancer challenge I asked myself the powerful question I had heard many times from Dr John Demartini: "If I were to die today would I say that I had done the best I could with everything I had?"

My answer was a resounding NO! I had some accomplishments. But I had not done my best.

One challenge I had had for as long as I remembered was thinking that I was not enough. I saw myself as inadequate and not sufficiently endowed to be successful. I had had big dreams and big goals for many years but, year after year, I did not succeed in getting any closer to any one of them.

For more than twenty years I had had the dream of becoming a bestselling author. I also dreamt of becoming a highly successful life coach, motivating and inspiring many people to become the best that they could be. I had high aspirations of becoming a highly successful entrepreneur through network marketing. I had deep desires to become financially free and to travel the world.

However, these dreams and goals remained unachieved mainly because I felt I was not good enough to achieve them. The dreams and goals were big and exciting in my imagination but unrealistic to my rational mind. I reasoned with myself that I was too small for such big dreams. I was not enough and I did not measure up. I had a deeply embedded belief that I was inadequate. That is why nothing ever happened and I never achieved any one of those dreams and goals.

Then I came face to face with my mortality. When I was told I had prostate cancer I found myself looking directly at death for the first time in my life. For a while a collision with this monster seemed imminent especially when I was told I had a stage four, aggressive type of prostate cancer. And who had ever survived a head-on collision with death dressed in an aggressive cancer? For the first few days my fate seemed sealed. The temptation to surrender mentally, emotionally, physically and spiritually was almost overwhelming.

However, the more I thought about my situation the more I felt I was not ready to die. In fact, it soon became very clear to me that I did not want to die. I wanted to live. I went into a bargaining mode of thinking. I told myself and God "If I got the chance to live again I would do the best I can with everything I had to make a positive difference and a positive impact on the world around me. I have to fight this aggressive cancer! But how do I do it? What chances do I have of surviving this fight against an enemy that appears so hugely formidable?"

It was my personal development background that came to the rescue. Right up to the present I sincerely believe that my life was saved by a statement. It was a statement I had read in many of the personal development books that I had read. It was a statement I had heard in quite a few of the personal development workshops and seminars I had attended. It was also a statement I had shared with my coaching clients. I had actually empowered quite a few of them with this statement. And the statement is "It is never what happens to you that defines and determines the quality of your life. It is your perception and how you respond to what happens to you."

I now felt deeply challenged to walk my talk and to live that statement. The more I thought about it the more I saw it as an opportunity and the more encouraged I felt. In that statement lay my potential to fight the prostate cancer and possibly win.

What that statement meant in my situation was that it was not my cancer status that I should allow to define and determine the quality of my life. Rather it was how I chose to perceive and respond to my cancer status that would determine the quality of my life –whether I was going to live a short or long life.

Just knowing that I had a choice was hugely empowering to me. At the back of my mind I knew that there was power in choice. And if I used that power wisely I would increase my chances and potential for survival.

With my back against the wall, I didn't have much of a choice and had nothing to lose by fighting with every weapon I had at my disposal.

For the first time since my diagnosis I realised that I had the potential to fight and win against the aggressive cancer that I faced. My greatest potential lay in the power of my mind. My mind was an extremely powerful weapon at my disposal. All I needed to do was, daily, deliberately and consciously decide to use it in ways that would have a positive impact on my life. I realised that with my mind I could choose attitudes that would increase my chances of survival against the cancer that had invaded my body.

What really boosted my morale was the realisation that I was actually not experiencing any pain yet from the cancer. It was just a diagnosis. Here was an opportunity that significantly increased my potential for survival. I was not feeling sick or ill. This fact alone gave me an incredible amount of physical, emotional, mental and spiritual energy to fight for dear life.

It soon became very clear in my mind that the more positive an attitude I adopted, the greater the chances of surviving the cancer. And the more positives and opportunities for winning that I identified, the greater potential I had to overcome the prostate cancer.

Another statement from my studies of personal development that came to my rescue says: "What you focus on expands", or "What you focus on is what you get". I figured out that if in the midst of my challenge I looked for opportunities and focused on them, that would significantly increase my chances and potential for survival. So I decided to focus on opportunities and believed that the more of them I came up with and the more time I spent thinking of them the more positive I would become, and the stronger my conviction for survival would be. That is exactly what I did and it actually worked for me.

Because of my personal development background and the power of my mind, as well as the fact that I was not actually sick, I began to identify other opportunities and blessings in my quest for survival.

I was a Christian and I believed in God and in the power of prayer. So I started to pray earnestly for myself. And I realised that the more positive my attitude was the more faith I had in God's presence in my life and the more energy and enthusiasm I put into my prayers. And strangely enough the more I prayed the more I believed that I would make it. My faith and prayer life significantly increased my potential for survival.

Living in Sydney at the time, I belonged to a charismatic and very prayerful group of Christians called the Servants of Jesus (SOJ) community. And when they heard of my prostate cancer diagnosis the whole community rallied together in prayer. They prayed for me as a congregation during Sunday services and also as individuals. One very prayerful leader of the community came to my place of residence and spent more than an hour with me in prayer.

This tremendous support significantly improved my attitude and confidence in my chances for survival. Being surrounded by such a community was in itself an opportunity that boosted my faith and potential for winning against the prostate cancer. It increased my faith in the power of prayer. It made the presence of God in my situation an empowering reality.

My wife and one of our daughters were studying natural therapy at the time and they gave me a lot of invaluable medical information on prostate cancer. They helped me see and appreciate the role and significance that natural therapy could play in the treatment of my condition. I was able to see that other options were available to me besides conventional medicine. I figured out that the more options I had the greater chances and potential I had for winning against the prostate cancer.

What also significantly increased my potential for survival was the availability of information. I went on the internet, visited libraries and bookshops and read as much as I could about prostate cancer. I reasoned with myself that if I could find people who had fought and won against prostate cancer, they would encourage me to fight and hopefully win my own battle.

My most prized find was a book titled "*How to Fight Prostate Cancer and Win*" by Ron Gellatley. This book, which I found in a bookshop within two weeks of my diagnosis, was my single biggest morale booster. I found the book to be a dynamo of positive thinking mixed with a lot of practical treatment suggestions. In this book Ron shared his own story of how he fought and won against prostate cancer.

This was exactly what I was looking for and I felt excited and extremely encouraged. I trusted Ron completely, not only because he had also been diagnosed with prostate cancer, but also because he was an accredited Naturopath, Clinical Nutritionist, Homeopath and Medical Herbalist. He had also been in medical practice for more than 15 years. I followed his recommendations for treatment to the letter.

I felt highly encouraged and inspired by Ron. I became significantly more confident about my chances of making it. My mindset and paradigm clearly shifted from fear to courage. I became more convinced than ever before that I could do it. My potential for winning against prostate cancer skyrocketed.

Embracing the opportunities and potential I had to overcome the prostate cancer gave me a new belief. When I started to believe that it was possible, I created a new reality that I did not have before. The reality was that I could play a significant role in healing myself. I felt highly empowered by this. This literally raised my energy levels. I needed as much energy as I could muster to give myself whatever chance I could to overcome the cancer that had invaded my body.

One important decision I made was to avoid taking myself too seriously. I decided that it was possible to create my own cheerful reality in spite of how grimly other people might see the situation. I decided that life was as serious or as light as I chose to see it.

I began to embrace the view that it was better to laugh at myself than to feel sorry for myself. It was better to make light of and laugh at situations around me than to take them too seriously. I chose to believe that my mind had the power and potential to heal me. I was going to create and look for as many opportunities as I could that empowered me to do so.

My general attitude became so positive that other people felt encouraged and inspired in my presence. I still clearly remember the comments from my family medical doctor on one of my many visits to her rooms. I was about to leave her consulting room after a session with her when she said to me: "I am really amazed by your attitude. Every time you come in here, you leave me feeling a lot better than when you came in. I am supposed to be the one to encourage and motivate you because of your medical condition, but it's always the other way around."

Even in the midst of some quite uncomfortable radiation therapy sessions I created situations that left me feeling encouraged and inspired. I found ways of cheering myself up.

After the first two radiation sessions, I decided to look for ways that could help me inject some positivity into the whole experience. During the first two sessions, I had noticed that once the radiation therapist had set me up for my treatment she left me all alone in this big room lying on my back and strapped on to a machine that was going to pump radiation into my body. She would go to another room where, a minute later, she would switch on the machine to begin treatment. The only company I had in that room was this machine that had three big metal heads that would swing or whirl around me once the machine was switched on.

During my third radiation session, and as soon as the therapist had left the room, I decided to personify the three metal heads and to talk to them. I believed that this would help to lighten my radiation therapy sessions. It would help me to not take things too seriously.

The first thing I did was to give names to the three metal heads. I determined each name based on the shape of the head or what it reminded me of. To the first head I gave the name, *Roundhead*. Respectively I called the second and the third, *Smiling Face* and *Flat Face*. I then did two things. Firstly, I introduced myself and explained my situation to them.

"Good day Roundhead, Smiling Face and Flat Face. You don't quite know me and so let me begin by introducing myself.

"My name is David and I am here because I need your help. I was recently diagnosed with an aggressive type of prostate cancer. What this means is that I am facing a real threat to my life from this cancer. Now I am here with you in this room because I believe that you can help me get rid of the malignant cancer cells that are threatening my life.

"I am not ready to die yet. I am here to buy time. I want to go on living because I still have a few big dreams I would still like to fulfill before I die. I believe I have the potential to be, to do and to have a lot more than my present life demonstrates. I still want to motivate and inspire tens of thousands of people – especially young people – to realise their full potential and to become the best that they can be. I have books and programmes to write and speeches to deliver. I have a much bigger legacy to leave behind. I am not done yet."

I then gave Roundhead, Smiling Face and Flat Face a pep talk, which I subsequently repeated during each session until the very end of my radiation therapy.

"Roundhead, Smiling Face and Flat Face, you know why I am here. I believe that you will help me realise my dreams. As I lie down here and close my eyes, I have complete faith and confidence that all will be well. I am grateful and I truly appreciate your presence and your help."

By the time I finished my radiation therapy sessions Roundhead, Smiling Face and Flat Face were like real people to me. I felt comfortable and relaxed as the radiation burrowed through my body, session after session. The psychological support I got from them gave my mind a light-hearted perception of an otherwise grim and heavy situation. It was a great boost to my growing faith and belief that I was going to overcome the cancer.

What was interesting and quite inspiring for me was the discovery that the high expectations and positive attitude that I now had about my healing had emanated from within. Potentially I had the power to significantly contribute towards my own healing. I had actually created the mindset that now dominated my thinking. There was a healer in me. It was quite clear that within me there was a power that I could use to deal with whatever challenge I faced. It was all about deciding to focus on the solutions and opportunities surrounding my challenging situation.

Becoming aware that I had the potential to fight and win against the cancer helped me realise that I also had a huge potential to be, do and have whatever I desired in this life. If I could successfully use the potential I had to survive the cancer, I could also identify and use the potential that I had to achieve my life's dreams and goals.

Knowing that I had an aggressive form of prostate cancer was, therefore, a powerful catalyst in getting me connected to the immense potential I had to fulfill my mission in life. Becoming aware of the power I had to contribute to my own physical healing helped me realise that I already had everything that it takes to live out my "short" life's purpose.

My new belief that I had a good fighting chance against prostate cancer gave me a new hope of a life after cancer. That actually became my new goal – to live beyond the cancer. I discovered that the more I focused on it the more believable it became to my mind and the greater potential I had of realising it.

How did I want to live my 'life after cancer'? Definitely, with greater focus and purpose. It was more imperative than ever before that I should clarify what my life was all about. I made a resolution and promised myself that I would do everything I could to live a more meaningful life, whether it was going to be a short or long life.

I became clearly aware that I would have no excuse, even if I died today, to say that I didn't have all that I needed to be the best that I could be and to make a positive difference in the world around me. I realised that I had always possessed everything I needed to be who I was meant to be. My potential had always been there. I had just been too lazy to challenge myself seriously enough. I had been too quick to find excuses and to live in the conviction of those excuses. I had found unproductive refuge in my comfort zone. It took me a life-threatening prostate cancer diagnosis to develop a new belief. I now believed in my potential to be, do and have anything that I truly wanted.

I now knew that the potential that I had would not be played out in my life unless I was willing to step out of my comfort zone and start playing the game. I had to dare go out there and do that which seemed daunting and challenging yet, at the same time connected with who I always wanted to be. Doing this would certainly give me a sense of fulfilment.

I had always wanted to be a leader and teacher of love and wisdom - leading, motivating and inspiring myself and others to be the best that we could be. This was how I wanted to make a positive difference in my own life and in the lives of as many people as I could touch.

This had been my dream and vision since 1995 when my wife and I got involved with a network marketing company as part-time distributors. I had never felt as highly inspired and connected to my dreams and goals as I felt working with this company. It was also my first ever business venture. Within three years we had made significant progress with the company including my public speaking involvement where I was giving business presentations on a regular basis. Unfortunately the company I was working with had to cease operations because of economic challenges in my country.

In 2001 I bought a franchise with an international personal and leadership development organisation. For five years I had provided and facilitated personal and leadership development programs for teenagers and adults. Over that period, and working with a business partner, I had positively impacted the lives of almost a thousand people, mostly teenagers. As far as my career was concerned, those five years had been the most fulfilling years of my entire working life of 26 years.

In February 2006, when I was 58, my life changed dramatically. For economic and political reasons my wife and I left my country of birth Zimbabwe and migrated to Australia. For the next five years I grappled and struggled with the issues of settling down in a new country. For most of that period I never held a permanent job and was content to do anything that put food on the table. I did casual teaching jobs, worked in and cleaned factories and also did quite a bit of voluntary work. My focus was on survival and I hardly had any time to think and reflect much on my long-term dreams and vision.

I had just got my first permanent job in Australia when I was diagnosed with prostate cancer in March 2011. I looked death in the face and found myself engaged in the biggest fight for life in the 63 years that I had lived. More than ever before I felt challenged to reflect on my life, its meaning, purpose, value and direction. I felt challenged to revisit and re-evaluate my dreams and goals.

I thought about my dream of becoming a writer. This was one way I had visualised myself living my desire to be a teacher of love and wisdom, through my books. And now here I was facing cancer and the possibility of dying and I had nothing to show for my writer's dream, not even a booklet.

I knew I could write and write well if I really put my mind to it. In my high school days, I had written some of the best essays in the classes I attended. I also had the experiences, wisdom and creativity needed to produce meaningful content, especially in the field of motivating and inspiring myself and other people to become the best that we can be. So I clearly had the potential to become a successful writer.

So, what was it that had stopped me? I had to be honest with myself. This was a defining moment and the truth had to be told. Procrastination and laziness had played a key role. As I reflected on my writing career I was disturbed to notice that I never finished any writing project that I had started. I could clearly see that since 2004 there were a few writing projects where I had started strong but then fizzled out and never finished.

And now as I faced prostate cancer and the possibility that I could die soon, I did not feel happy at all with myself as a writer. In fact, I had no right to call myself a writer. I had nothing at all published in my name. If I was to face my death right now what would I say about my big writing dream? I would certainly not tell myself that I had done the best I could with everything I had. The truth was that I had not used the full potential that I had as a writer at all. I had been dreaming big and talking big to myself and other people about being a writer, but after almost eight years I had nothing to show for it. I certainly had not walked my talk. I felt a deep pain and disappointment with myself.

I literally prayed for another lease on life. I asked for a second chance. I vowed to myself and to God that if I got another chance to live I would do everything I could to write the story of my life and most certainly the story of my experience with prostate cancer. I would use my story as a source of encouragement and inspiration for myself and other people.

Since moving to Australia in 2006 I had increasingly seen myself living a meaningful and fulfilling life as a coach. In 2009, I had obtained a qualification as a certified life coach. I knew I had the gift of listening to people and helping them see their challenges from a new and empowering perspective. I knew that I could motivate and inspire people – especially teenagers and young adults – to become the best that they could be. However, since becoming a qualified life coach in 2009 I had not moved with any sense of urgency towards establishing myself as a coach. In fact, I wasn't so sure any more that coaching would be a career I needed to focus on and take seriously.

Then prostate cancer struck. As I faced the prospect of dying, I found myself asking so many questions for which I had to find answers. My life depended on it. The quality of the answers I came up with could save my life. In fact, I felt quite empowered by some of the answers that came up.

There were quite a few questions that at first seemed to have no answers. Then when I persisted and focused on the question long enough, answers began to surface. One particular question I asked myself when I drew a blank in trying to deal with a challenge was: "If I knew what the answer was, what would it be?" The most interesting and empowering development from this was that an answer always surfaced where I had told myself: "I don't know. I have no answer for this." Every problem had a solution. Every question had an answer

One realisation soon hit me. The kind of questions I was asking myself were so similar to the questions that I had been asking my clients. My prostate cancer challenge had turned me into my own coach. My survival depended on how well I was going to coach myself. This connected very well with the idea I have looked at earlier: "Becoming my own best friend." For me to become my own best friend, I had to become my own best coach and mentor. Before I could effectively coach anyone else out there I had to coach myself well first.

I was very excited about this discovery and I made a very important decision. I was going to coach myself through my prostate cancer challenge and if I survived, I would commit to remain a coach for the rest of my life. I would not only be a life coach for myself. I would also be a coach for other people. If I could successfully coach and empower myself through my prostate cancer challenge, I could do the same for other people. I certainly had the potential to be a good coach for both myself and other people. There was no better way to walk my talk than to model my coaching of other people on my coaching of myself. The coaching models and processes I had seen working in my own life, I could confidently use with other people.

My prostate cancer diagnosis also awakened the speaker in me. As I navigated my way through this life-threatening reality, I increasingly realised that if ever I was going to survive the challenge, I would have a story to tell. I was also beginning to feel convinced that I had accumulated a lot of wisdom over the 63 years that I had lived.

I knew that some people would benefit from the wisdom I had gathered through my life's experiences. During the 37 years that I had worked as a teacher, headmaster, youth coach and adviser, I had spoken to thousands of students during my classes, school assemblies, youth meetings and facilitation sessions. Many of these young people had expressed appreciation for the wisdom that I had shared with them. Some that I had met years later as adults had gone so far as to say that I had positively inspired them to achieve the success that they were now experiencing.

Clearly my speeches had made a positive impact. I had the potential to motivate and inspire people through public speaking. And so I decided that in addition to writing, speaking was going to be one of the ways I was going to share my story and my wisdom.

I realised that the very gift of life that I had and that I had previously taken so much for granted, was itself a huge potential asset that I needed to maximise to achieve all the dreams that I had. I was capable of achieving my dreams because I was alive. If the death that now threatened me became a reality, there would be no dreams to talk about. The writer, coach and speaker in me would also die prematurely without seeing the light of day. It made a lot of sense for me to use all the potential that I had to make a positive difference in my own life and in the lives of many other people.

Above all, it was believing that I had the potential to heal myself that gave me the courage and determination to do so. I believed I could do it and I did it. It gave me the courage to take the necessary action. It compelled me to act positively. That is how the power of this potential worked for me.

It took eighteen months for me to become prostate cancer free. Medically, it took radiation therapy,and naturopathic and homeopathic treatment. Spiritually, it took a lot of prayers and a very high level of faith on my part. Above all, throughout my treatment I chose to adopt a positive attitude and a strong belief that I had the potential, born of my unique identity, to heal myself and help make that freedom possible.

In less than two years after becoming cancer free another gift and talent surfaced in my life. In February 2014, I discovered the **songwriter** in me. I have written more than thirty songs, most of which I have taught to hundreds of young people since then. I have a huge potential to grow in this area.

More than five years after the diagnosis, I am still prostate cancer free. I sincerely believe that the positive mindset and attitudes that I adopted played a major role in my healing. And one key attitude was believing that I had the potential to positively influence the results that I eventually achieved.

Because that belief helped me with the prostate cancer challenge, I have adopted it to deal with any other challenges that have confronted me since 2011. I have used it to deal with the business, financial, relationship and family challenges that I have encountered. I have used it in dealing with the challenges of relocating from Australia to South Africa. And every time, without fail, it has worked for me.

In fact, it has brought me to a place where I sincerely believe that I have the potential to be, to do and to have whatever I seriously desire and commit myself to achieving.

 And it can do the same for you as well. When you acknowledge that you have the potential and capacity to deal with whatever challenges you face, you significantly increase your chances of doing so. It is all about convincing yourself: "I can do it!" When you constantly repeat these four short words to yourself and reflect on your God-given potential you are more than halfway there.

From my experiences, I have come to a place of total belief that whatever challenge I face, I have an inbuilt potential to find solutions to and overcome that challenge. I also believe that every challenge comes with lessons to learn and grow. I don't just believe that about myself. I believe that about every human being.

Affirmations: I HAVE POTENTIAL

- *I have gifts and talents that no one else has in exactly the same way I have them.*
- *I have within me everything I need to be, to do and to have anything I want.*
- *I am using my potential to the full so that I can become the best that I can be.*
- *I can dream big dreams and I have the potential to act big and achieve big.*
- *I am doing the best I can with everything I have to make a positive difference.*
- *I have the potential to fight and win against any challenges which come my way.*
- *I am choosing to use my unlimited potential to live the life of my dreams.*
- *I raise my potential for greater success by embracing the gifts and talents that I have.*
- *I can create whatever attitude and mindset I choose in order to maximise my potential.*
- *I focus on my gifts and talents and the potential I have to fulfill my life's mission.*
- *I choose to step out of my comfort zone so that I realise my full potential.*
- *I have the potential to see and use powerful life lessons in every challenge I face.*

CHAPTER 6

I AM BIGGER THAN MY PROBLEMS

Rather than shrinking away from your problems, grow bigger than them.
Zig Ziglar

You can call them problems or challenges
Disturbing messengers of what life arranges
Looking larger than life and wielding intimidation
Convincingly menacing tricksters of imitation
Making you believe they're firmly in control

Led by Captain Fear they march in formation
Doubt ,worry and anxiety conveying information
That they're here to stay and your fate is sealed
That you'd better give up and make fear your shield
That you've no control – it belongs to problems

You can't touch or see them – totally invisible
Convincingly present and seemingly invincible
They tower your life making you look so small
They've power over you, they've power to kill
Focus on them and they swallow your life.

It is your mind that feeds and breeds them
It is your mind with the power to shrink them
Reverse the focus and highlight your power
Take your rightful place you are the tower
Problems are visitors don't give them power

Take back your pride and reclaim your freedom
Take back control of your life and your kingdom
Love and feed yourself, happiness is your right
Starve your problems to death and win the fight
Don't give them control – your life belongs to you

You are much bigger than any of your problems
Give yourself energy and don't feed your problems
Power belongs to you and not your problems
Give yourself authority and boot out your problems
Their role is to serve you, they're meant to grow you

During the first few days of my diagnosis the cancer would loom large in my mind, intimidating and overwhelming. It was easier for me to imagine things going wrong rather than right. It was easier to conjure up images of disaster rather than victory over the cancer.

For many days after my diagnosis the cancer was certainly dominating my thinking, my behaviour and my entire life. It looked like a big black evil cloud that was descending lower and lower from the sky like an eagle that had spotted its prey. And it was swooping straight down on me with the evil intention of taking my life away. I pictured myself growing smaller and smaller and eventually getting swallowed by this monster. This image terrified my thoughts during the day and dominated my dreams at night.

I felt small. I felt helpless. I felt totally vulnerable. At first, I saw cancer as a merciless ravaging beast that was too big and too powerful for me to do anything about. Its mission was to kill and it had decimated hundreds of thousands of lives from time immemorial. It had targetted me and decided that I was its next death row victim.

Who was I and what could I do once this monster had targetted me? I was insignificantly small and vulnerable. At first it seemed easier to give in rather than try to put up a futile fight and engage in a fruitless battle which I stood no chance of winning. I looked at the cancer that had invaded my body with fear and reverence, as if it had the blessings of God or the Universe. Death by prostate cancer seemed to be clearly my ordained fate. God and prostate cancer had collaborated. In fact, at first, prostate cancer appeared to be a messenger sent by God. From every angle and in every respect my fate seemed signed, sealed and decided. Why and how was I going to argue with that?

I also focused my mind on the many people I knew that had died of cancer including prostate cancer. I spent hours vividly recalling visiting some of them in hospital and others in their homes. The pain on their faces spoke volumes of what was going on in their bodies. Looking at their shrunken bodies and seeing them in great pain had also been a painful experience for me that often brought tears to my own eyes. And when they had eventually died, unrecognisable skeletons of their former selves, it had brought relief to them, their loved ones and to me as well.

I also spent time mentally revisiting some of the friends and relatives' funerals that I had attended. At times, my imagination would run wild and I would play a movie of my own funeral. My own funeral now became a larger reality in my mind than it had ever been in my life before. Death, most certainly, looked bigger than life.

I spent hours on end thinking about my two late brothers, Charles and Edward, both victims of cancer. I could vividly picture them in my mind. They were like messengers of death, making it clear to me that my end was just as certain and inescapable as theirs had been. For a while it seemed as if, in their spiritual world, they were conspiring to hasten my death. It felt as if they were anxious for me to join them. How could I ignore their brotherly messages?

I clearly remembered Charles wasting away as a result of a long battle with cancer. By the time he died, he had shrunk into a tiny, unrecognisable skeletal shadow of his former self. I vividly recalled that his wife Elizabeth who had nursed him in his long illness, suddenly died on the very same day her husband died. It was a double family tragedy. More than 20 years later I still remembered the family trauma, tears and fears that accompanied the double funeral.

Edward, who was older than Charles, died while on a visit to Australia. A few weeks earlier he and his wife had happily bid us farewell and flown off to visit their children. Shortly after arriving in Australia he fell ill. The diagnosis was a very advanced stomach cancer that had already spread to many other parts of the body. He died within days and arrived back home in a coffin. The shock and stress was too much for my mind and body and I had collapsed as we were collecting his body from the undertakers for burial.

And now it was my turn. I felt scared, recalling the deaths of my two brothers. I had been told that cancer was hereditary. Clearly it ran in our family and had now caught up with me. How many days, or weeks or months was it before my own funeral came up?

For a while worry, doubt and fear seemed the most natural responses to my situation. At times, I felt so anxious and depressed that it seemed the wisest thing to do was to just give up and let fate take its course. My fate seemed clear for all to see. I had undergone some blood tests and it was scientifically established that my body was afflicted by a "terminal" disease known as prostate cancer. What this meant to me at the time was that an irreversible and accelerated physical disintegration of my body had been set in motion by those malignant cancer cells. Thinking that I was going to live seemed so illogical and senseless.

As a Christian, I remembered vividly the words from the 'Book of Ecclesiastes': "To everything there is a season, a time for every purpose under heaven: A time to be born, and a time to die." I saw death as an integral part of life and I felt that my "time to die" had come.

If it wasn't for the fact that I was a life coach and a Christian surrounded by people praying for me all the time, I'm convinced that the cancer would have had a field day with me. It would have grown bigger and bigger and eventually run my life down to the grave.

As a life coach, I started to ask myself the very same questions that I used to ask my clients. One question was "How was I choosing to see the challenging situation that I faced? Was I choosing to see it positively or negatively?"

The other question I asked myself was: "Even if I was going to die in the very near future, in what state of mind did I want to die?" Did I want to die in a state of fear, misery, sadness and depression or did I want to die feeling happy, excited, positive and highly expectant of my life after death?

Did I want to die feeling small, scared and completely cowed down by the prostate cancer? No! I would rather die in courage and confidence, looking straight-faced at the cancer that was taking my life away.

Clearly, I didn't want to die miserable, sad and depressed. If at all possible, I preferred to die happy, excited and looking forward to a heavenly existence after death. This led me to a reflection of what kind of an illness I wanted to experience. I had never thought of this before. I had just assumed that if anybody was sick or ill, it was an automatic call for them to feel miserable, unhappy and depressed. I had never associated happiness with illness. I began to realise for the first time in my entire life that it was actually possible to choose to be happy even when I was ill.

As a Christian, I was deeply encouraged by the people who were praying for me. While I was initially confronting God and asking him why he had allowed the cancer to invade my body, they were encouraging me by continuously telling me that God loved me and wanted me to live. And when I started focusing on how God was loving me, it didn't take me long to actually start seeing how I was indeed being loved.

These people who were praying for me had the most sincere human will and desire for me to live. After all, their prayers were focused on asking God to heal me. They were injecting a positive spirit and energy into my life. So why would I think and behave in a negative way that would contradict that spirit?

Once I started to see God on my side it helped me to start entertaining the possibilities of being bigger than the cancer. For me God was the greatest power in the universe, in the whole of creation. Therefore, being on the same side with him was an enormous morale booster. What if I could give God the benefit of the doubt? What if I chose to believe that God was using the cancer to help me grow my faith in him? What if the cancer was meant to leave me a stronger person? The more I inclined my thinking in this direction, the more I felt spiritually and psychologically empowered to boldly face and fight the cancer.

After spending some time imagining the worst and allowing the cancer to intimidate me, the coach in me surfaced. I started to realise that I actually had some choices and big decisions to make. I had to choose how I wanted to look at the cancer that had invaded my body. I had the choice of allowing the cancer to dominate the situation and to appear bigger than my own life. I could have very easily looked at the cancer as a big black cloud that had come to take my life away. I could have allowed the cancer to intimidate me and to run my life.

On the other hand, I could choose not to allow the cancer to intimidate me and to run my life. I could choose to fight the cancer with everything I had, especially my faith in God and a positive mindset. Although quite a big challenge, it was also possible for me to choose to see myself as being bigger than the cancer and to allow that attitude to influence my thinking and behaviour.

As a life coach I had encountered clients who came to see me because they were facing challenges in their lives. I had always encouraged them with these words: "It is never what happens to you but how you respond that determines the quality and direction of your life." I had challenged them to respond positively. They did and it had always worked for them.

Now it was time for me to walk my talk. And as I faced prostate cancer my clients' testimonies became very powerful sources of encouragement for me. I was now using their experiences to coach myself. In a strange new twist of events my clients had become my coaches. I asked myself this question: "If my clients knew about my prostate cancer condition, what would they say to me?" I knew for certain that they would encourage me to fight for my life and health.

I was sure that my clients would tell me: "Never give up! Take charge and fight on up to the end. Never let your problems take over your life!" They would simply be reflecting back to me the words of encouragement that I had often shared with them. The more I recalled our coaching sessions together and the discussions we had, the more positive voices I heard and the more encouraged I felt.

My spiritual life also played a significant role in empowering me to successfully deal with the prostate cancer challenge that I faced. As a Catholic Christian I believed in prayer and communicated with my God regularly. During my prayer sessions, I often read my Bible and always tried to find some relevance between what I read and where my life was.

For the first few days after my diagnosis I found it very hard to pray. I had a lot of questions for God. Why had he allowed that to happen? Why me? What had I done wrong to deserve that? I was very upset and angry with Him. My faith in God was shaken to its very foundation.

It was also through the people who prayed for me and in my Bible readings and prayers that I felt the reality of God's presence in my life. Having been told that I had an aggressive type of prostate cancer, I believed that only a miracle would save my life. And for me only God, only Jesus Christ was the source of that miracle. Only with faith was any healing miracle possible.

I learnt at the time that the opposite of faith was fear. I had to choose whether I was going to live with faith or fear. Once I was consciously aware that I had to make a choice, fear was not an option. I became convinced and chose to believe that as long I had faith and desired to be healed everything was possible with God.

Besides belonging to my Catholic parish I was also part of an ecumenical Christian community called *"The Servants of Jesus (SOJ)."* By the time I was diagnosed with prostate cancer my wife and I had been part of this community for three years. The Servants of Jesus was an extremely caring community that had played a very significant role in helping us settle in Sydney, Australia, where we had relocated from Zimbabwe in 2006. They had provided us with spiritual, emotional, social and material support that had made a big positive difference in our lives.

The SOJ community also provided tremendous spiritual and emotional support when I was diagnosed with prostate cancer. They openly prayed for me during our Sunday services. One senior member of the community spent a considerable amount of time praying for and with me at my home.

The clear message I got from the people who prayed for me and from my own spiritual reflections was how critically important it was for me to believe that God would heal me. I was challenged to grow in faith. I had a powerful encounter with the power of choice. What was I going to choose to believe – that I would be healed or that I would not be healed? It seemed at the time that I had to make a choice between life and death. What was I going to allow to dominate my mind – thoughts of life or thoughts of death? Thoughts of death were dark, depressing and filled with despair. Thoughts of life were positive, encouraging and filled with hope.

It was towards the end of the first week after receiving the prostate cancer verdict that I decided I would rather entertain thoughts of life as much as I could. I decided to fight hard to keep away depressing thoughts of death.

I started to notice that it was during those calm moments when I allowed my God and the coach in me to speak that I would then ask myself some empowering questions. This often led to long conversations with myself during which my God and the "coach" would convince me that it was possible to survive the cancer. Talking to myself proved to be the most powerful healing force as I faced my long fight with cancer.

When I had exaggerated thoughts of an impending doom and death, this drove me to extremes of depression, fear, doubt, worry and anxiety. What if I reversed this trend and focused my thoughts on successfully fighting the prostate cancer and then travelling the world visiting my children and having fun with my grandchildren? Why not grow the picture and image of one day becoming completely free of cancer once again? I'd rather fill my life with positive thoughts than negative ones. Such thinking became more and more common and also welcome.

I became more and more aware that I had the choice of either empowering the cancer or empowering myself. This was a significant improvement from my initial position where the only option I had seen was giving in to the cancer. From a position of powerlessness, I began to feel empowered. The vision of being bigger than the cancer became more and more believable to my mind.

The attitudes that I was going to choose as I fought this challenge would determine the kind of relationship I was choosing to have with the cancer. If I chose to adopt the idea that I was a victim and entertained self- pity, I would be inviting fear, sadness, and a lot of frustrations into my life. The cancer would loom large, intimidating and overwhelming and I would grow smaller and smaller and eventually get swallowed by it. If I chose this attitude, I would be behaving as my own worst enemy.

Was I going to give the cancer energy, power, authority and control or was I going to claim the energy, power, authority and control myself? Was I going to allow the cancer to be bigger than I was and to intimidate me into submission? I asked myself: "Is the cancer going to run my life or am I going to be in charge?" Once again, I had to make a choice.

I refused to give the cancer energy, power, authority and control. I decided that energy, power, authority and control over this matter belonged to me. No one was going to give these sources of psychological power to me. I would have to claim them. After all this was my life. If I gave up control, I would be giving up my life. I was not ready to do that yet.

After all, I believed in a God who was bigger than any human problem. He certainly was bigger than my prostate cancer. Could he not help me to feel and see myself bigger than the cancer as well?

I decided that I was going to be bigger than the prostate cancer that had invaded my body. I was going to stand up to it. I was not going to cowardly lie there, submit to it and surrender my life. I was not going to beg for my life. My life was not just for the taking. I was going to fight for it. The idea of seeing myself bigger than the cancer suggested to me that I could have a psychological advantage over the challenge I was facing. Seeing myself bigger than the cancer or any problem I faced would give me some energy, power, authority and control to fight whatever problem confronted me. This was actually a good way to face life's challenges, which, after all, were inevitable.

What I needed to do was singularly focus on adopting and maintaining a positive attitude. This was key and would enable me to continue to generate the energy, power, authority and control that I desperately needed in my fight against the cancer enemy.

However, what was very clear to me was that to have any chance of winning the fight, I needed some allies. The enemy was too big for me to face by myself.

Clearly God was my first ally. I believed in him and saw him as a power bigger than any other power that I had encountered in my 63-odd years of existence in this world.

However, God was spiritual. I needed some allies that I could relate with at the human level. Who would provide me with the empathy, support and encouragement that I needed? It would have to be people who had a full understanding of the challenge that I faced.

And so I chose to look for people who had faced cancer, fought it and won. I researched , bought books and spent time reading about these people and how they had done it. This is how I came across Ron Gelantley's book "*How to Fght Prostate Cancer and Win*." As already indicated in an earlier chapter Ron became my human hero and role model in my own fight against prostate cancer. He became a perfect example to me of someone who chose to be bigger than his problems.

I decided that as I went through my treatment programme I was going to spend as much time as I could exposing myself to positive influences. I said to myself "If I am going to die from this cancer I'd rather die smiling." Yes I chose to be bigger than the cancer itself.

I chose to be grateful for the gift of life and health and to focus on my strengths and on the opportunities I had to overcome this challenge.

What also helped me significantly was the decision I made to look at the challenge I faced as temporary. I chose to see it as a temporary intrusion and passing phase. Generally, I had always enjoyed good health and had proudly regarded myself as a healthy person. In my entire life I had been hospitalised only once for a minor surgical procedure. So the malignant prostate cancer cells that were growing in my healthy body could be defeated. After all I was not really experiencing any pain. It was nothing more than "just a diagnosis". My healthy body was much bigger than the malignant cancer cells. I could use this body to fight the cancer and win. The more I focused on this mindset, the bolder and more confident I felt against the cancer.

I chose to be bigger than the cancer. I decided to take 100 percent responsibility for all the decisions that would come into my treatment program. I was not going to surrender anything about my life to the cancer or to anyone else. I realised that whether I made the wrong decision or the right decision, the power to make that decision was mine. The cancer was a servant and I was the master. That empowering distinction was key for me.

By deciding to take full responsibility for everything that was going to happen to me I was preventing the cancer itself from dictating the quality of my life. I was giving myself the greatest gift possible under the circumstances. By deciding to make the best of each moment that I was alive, I was raising the quality of my life to levels I had never enjoyed before. I felt highly empowered seeing my huge giant mental-self towering over my small scared problem.

I realised that while life was full of challenges, the difference between those who succeeded in life and those who didn't was in how they looked at their challenges. It was all in the way they perceived their problems. It was all in how they chose to relate to the inevitable problems that life occasionally threw at them. Were they choosing to allow their problems to intimidate them? Were they allowing those problems to balloon out of proportion in their minds? Were they finding themselves shrinking smaller and smaller in the face of their problems?

Seeing myself bigger than the prostate cancer was a significant accomplishment. It was a game changer for me that I had been empowered to face that challenge with boldness. I had made a decision to stay on top of the situation. The experience gave me a new road map for dealing with future challenges. Whether I was going to face health, financial, relationship, social, spiritual or business challenges, I decided I was going to see myself bigger than my problems.

I chose not to focus on my problems any more and not to spend time entertaining them. My problems didn't deserve that. I was no longer going to invite them to intimidate me. I was no longer going to sink so low as to beg my problems to spare my life. Doing that would be giving my problems energy, power, authority and control over my life.

I decided instead to give myself the energy, power, authority and control over my life. I decided to expand myself and to become bigger than my problems. I decided to focus on my dreams and strengths. I chose to hold on to any thought or idea that made me look better and stronger than my problems. I chose to believe that I could always overcome my challenges. And that is what manifested in my life, especially in my fight against prostate cancer.

When I decided to take charge and to take control I became my own very best friend. I became my own hero. I became bigger than my problems and the possibility of overcoming my cancer challenge received another boost.

Affirmations: I AM BIGGER THAN MY PROBLEMS

- *I am bigger than the problems and challenges that come my way.*
- *I have the power to choose how I want to look at each of my problems.*
- *I choose to look down and not up at each of my problems.*
- *I see problems and solutions as two sides of the same coin.*
- *I choose daily to focus on the side of solutions and I watch my problems shrink and get smaller.*
- *I choose to see problems as mentors that have come to strengthen me.*

- *I daily use my power of choice and I choose to be bigger than my problems.*
- *I grow bigger than my problems as I choose to focus on my faith rather than my fears.*
- *I choose to empower myself rather than empower my problems.*
- *I choose to give energy, authority and control to myself and not to my problems.*
- *I am winning over my problems. I'm always defeating them.*
- *I choose to outstare my poblems and get them to submit to my authority and control.*
- *I am a huge giant towering over my small scared and cowardly problems.*

CHAPTER 7

I LIVE IN ABUNDANCE

"Nothing is impossible to the mind. All its guidance and power are available to you. When you have fully realised THOUGHT CAUSES ALL, there will never be any limits that you yourself do not impose."
U S Andersen

Know your source and you'll know your strength
Know that your source has no breadth and length
Beyond your mother's womb is a connecting code
Leading to your ultimate creator's umbilical code
Endlessly long, invisibly strong, stretching to eternity

You're born of abundance, an extension of the boundless.
You're a child of infinity and your potential is endless
With the wealthiest parentage your'e enormously gifted
Your home is abundance and your supply unlimited
Born of a deathless soul you've an abundant identity

You were born to create like your boundless creator
You've an abundant imagination, you're a co-creator
From an abundance of causes just choose your mission
There are dreams galore – connect with your vision
As a partner with the universe your support is endless

I dare you to dream, imagine and create with abandon
Conspire with your source and embrace your abundance
Think big, as much as you want, your mind won't burst
Create the idea, focus your willpower, imagine your best
Let your wildest dreams become your wildest reality

You've everything you need to be anything you choose
Get excited, hold to your choice, you've nothing to lose
Whatever you purpose you possess gifts and talents
That are abundantly present, as your dreams' parents
Birthing them to reality, bringing great joy in abundance

From abundance you came and in abundance you live
You are abundantly gifted so that you abundantly give
Walk an abundant life's journey of unlimited experience
Let abundance light your path with showers of radiance
Fulfill your purpose, live in abundance, it is your destiny

When I received the news of my cancer diagnosis, I went into depression. I experienced a hopelessness and helplessness that drained me of all energy. The sun set in my life and I plunged into darkness. Whatever lights had ever shone in my life were rapidly switching off. Death seemed an irrefutable certainty. It was just a matter of time.

The light of life went out inside me. I thought of nothing except death. I felt deprived not only of life, but also of happiness, joy and opportunities. There was no reason to smile, let alone laugh. I saw the big dreams I had entertained being snatched away from me. All the good that life ever held for me was fast fading away. Mentally, physically and spiritually I was suffocating. I was fast running out of air.

For the first five days, I felt completely empty and unworthy. I had this overwhelming feeling that I was losing my life. Everything had become meaningless. It felt as though there was nothing left for me in this world. The diagnosis seemed to be making a big statement that my days were now numbered. It felt like I was no longer welcome in this world.

Was it really worth living anymore? Was my life's journey coming to an end? Was this my time to die?

As I allowed thoughts of death and deprivation to dominate my life, I completely lost my sense of appreciation. Even when people prayed, said or did anything positive for me, it all sounded and felt lifeless and insincere. It felt as if the human side of me and my positive mindset were also dying.

By the fifth day, I was beginning to feel ill and starting to tell myself that I was suffering from prostate cancer. However, if anyone was to ask me what kind of physical pain I was experiencing, I wouldn't have been able to tell them. I had no physical pain. It was all in my mind. And it seemed as though my mind was now telling my body to acknowledge and start experiencing illness. Was this the mind-body connection that I had heard and read about? What was I doing to myself?

When the realisation hit me that I was not in physical pain and that it was only a diagnosis, my perspective started to change. The first thing I became aware of was how negatively powerful my mind had become. By just entertaining the fear of death from cancer, I had created a death-smelling chamber of horrors for myself. I had spent hours on end entertaining nothing but negative depressing thoughts.

And the most chilling realisation was that the more I had entertained negative thoughts, the more of a reality they became. I had driven myself to feeling ill. And who knows - if I had carried on along that negative path, I would have become a welcome ally to the active cancer cells in my body. I would have plunged my immune system to rock bottom. The cancer cells in my body would have had a field day and I would have driven myself prematurely into an early grave.

The most powerful lesson I learned from my initial negative experiences was the realisation that my mind was the most powerful weapon I had as I faced prostate cancer. It became crystal clear to me that if I used my mind positively it would give me positive results. Likewise, if I used it negatively, as I had done so far, it would give me negative results.

If I had created such a negative life-threatening mindset within a few days, I equally had the potential to also create a highly positive life-supporting mindset. If I had been able to build a growing arsenal of negative thoughts and circumstances, I must also have the capacity to create a host of positive thoughts and reasons why I should go on living. If I had been able to invite and allow thoughts of death and scarcity to start running my life, I could also invite thoughts of life and abundance to dominate my whole existence.

It dawned on me that even if I was going to die soon, it would be better to die with an abundance of positive thoughts than with a lot of fear and negative thoughts in my mind. What an empowering realisation!

What a discovery! I could actually use the power of my mind to help me heal myself. What if the mind-body connection was actually a reality? Why not use my prostate cancer situation to find out? What if it worked out? My entire life depended on it. Even if I died while trying to harness the power of my mind for my own healing, I would have died an honourable death. I would have greater self-respect. It would be better to die with a positive mindset than with a negative one. I had nothing to lose.

Once I got a handle on the power and potential that I had to heal myself, I did not want to let go. I had made a life-changing discovery for myself. I was abundantly rich. My mind was a billion dollar asset if only I could bring myself to sincerely believe it; if only I could master how to use it in a positive way. Instead of entertaining limiting thoughts and beliefs about my prostate cancer status I had to start looking for, and entertaining empowering thoughts and beliefs about my life and situation.

All this was happening on a foundation of faith in a God of abundance to whom I prayed every day. After the diagnosis and in the midst of my fears, I prayed more than I had ever prayed before. I felt lost and I needed God's guidance on how I was going to navigate my way through this greatest challenge of my life. I had initially blamed and was angry with God for my cancer status. I had many moments of doubt and sceptism about God's availability to me at this my hour of greatest need.

However, in spite of my anger, fear, doubt and scepticism outside of God there was no other power greater than myself that I could go to at this challenging time. There was no one else out there I could lean on and feel secure with. It was only when I started to connect God with my positive mindset that everything began to fall into place. Once I stopped blaming him for the cancer challenge that I faced and started to see him as the source of all that was good in my life, I began to see more and more of his presence.

God had everything to do with the first positive reality - that I was not sick. I had no physical pain. I needed to capitalise on this. This would enable me to muster whatever physical, mental and creative energies I needed to fight the prostate cancer. Had the diagnosis come at a time when I was already sick, it would have been a completely different ball game. I would have been more justified in feeling hopeless and helpless.

Was this God's perfect timing playing out in my life? Was it true that there were no coincidences in life? Could it be true that everything happened for a reason? What if the prostate cancer diagnosis had happened at the time and in the way that it did for a good reason? What if it was all meant to enhance the quality of my own life and health?

What if the diagnosis was a timeous warning that came at a time when the growing cancer cells had not yet caused irreversible damage to my body? Maybe this was an opportunity for me to fight the cancer and succeed before it had become too powerful. Could it be that God was giving me a second chance and wanted me to grow from the experience? Was it possible that God was trying to tell me that he loved me and was doing so through the prostate cancer experience?

All these thoughts and questions were filled with seeds of abundance. They led me to see many positive things in my cancer situation.

It began to make a lot of sense for me to start building a case against the cancer rather than building a case against my own chances of living. The more I saw God on my side, the easier this became. I felt less bitter and more appreciative of the gifts that began to unfold before my eyes.

Not only did I have the gift of health. I was also alive, breathing in and out. I was not dead. I was not feeling any pain. All it meant was that some active cancer cells were starting to grow in my body. My challenge was to put up a fight; to prevent these intruder cells from spreading. I had to stop them from advancing to a point where they would inflict pain on my body and eventually death. I was now at war and would have to fight many battles. And I had discovered my most powerful weapons – my positive mindset and an abundant God.

I had taken the precious gifts of life and health for granted. In fact ,by initially being as negative as I had been, I had completely ignored these amazing gifts.

At that point another powerful awareness hit me. Whoever I wanted to be, whatever I wanted to do and have in this world, life and health were the foundation. Whatever challenges I faced, if I could tick life and health – if I had them, I had a good chance of successfully dealing with those challenges. And they were not just amazing gifts, they were incredible blessings. For me they formed a solid foundation for the abundant gifts and blessings that I began to see around me. With these newly discovered gifts of life and health, I could do anything. They triggered in my mind a creative process that unearthed an abundance of positive and supportive situations. And these situations would become a source of courage and inspiration in my battle with prostate cancer.

The next positive reality I became aware of was the amount of support I had as I faced my prostate cancer challenge. My wife and my children were extremely supportive. And then there was my church community. They took the time to dedicate a part of a worship session to pray for me. A senior member of the church visited my home and spent over an hour praying for and counselling me.

I also got a lot of support from my workplace. My manager at work took time to discuss my situation with me and assured me that she was available for me if I needed any help.

Then there was my family doctor and my oncologist. I had also decided to work with a naturopath and a homoeopath in my battle with cancer. I certainly had an abundance of support. This was an encouraging and supportive environment. I had every reason to be grateful and positive about my situation.

Thinking of and appreciating the support I had prompted me to ask myself: "What other support can

I create for myself so that I can generate more positive energy around me?" Throughout my life I had always loved reading books, especially in my number one area of interest – personal development.

Now having been diagnosed with prostate cancer brought the subject of cancer right up on par with personal development as an area of interest. This is how I came across Ron Gelantely's book "*How to Fight Prostate Cancer and Win.*" This soon became my top companion. For a week or two after finding this book I could not put it down. I felt abundantly blessed and inspired reading it.

This book had an abundance of encouragement and advice on how I could fight and win against the prostate cancer that had invaded my body. I was reading the most inspiring, motivating and encouraging information from someone who had actually gone through what I was going through. Ron Gelantely had been diagnosed with an even more aggressive type of prostate cancer than mine. He had fought the cancer and succeeded. Not only was he encouraging me that it could be done. In his book he was telling me exactly how he had done it and the medicines and supplements that he had used.

Ron became real in my life. He became the closest companion that I walked with for quite a while on my journey with cancer. I followed every piece of advice he gave me in his book. The many treatment and lifestyle suggestions he made abundantly blessed my life. Emotionally and spiritually I felt at peace with myself. I was deeply grateful to God for bringing him into my life.

I also found support groups for people with cancer and specifically prostate cancer on the internet. There were quite a few websites where people were sharing their experiences and some very sound and helpful advice. I certainly had an abundance of support. I was not alone and felt encouraged that I could face the cancer and succeed. This was a big boost to my positive mindset.

Just having access to the internet made me realise how blessed I was. I had at my disposal an abundantly rich source of information. All I needed to do was just go to Google and type in whatever issue I needed information about regarding my cancer condition. I got the information I was looking for,but every time I went through this process I would come up with a lot of other very helpful information that I would never have known about. And usually this incidental information would prove to be even more useful than what I was originally looking for.

One area where the internet proved to be a highly valuable source of information was with the prescriptions I got from my oncologist and also my family doctor. Both my wife and my daughter, who were studying alternative medicine, had made me aware of the fact that virtually all prescribed medicine that I got from the pharmacist had side effects. They had advised me that whenever I got a prescription from my doctor and before I bought the medication, it would help me to Google whatever drug it was to find out more about its side effects.

I remember one particular prescription that I was given by my oncologist. This prescription was meant to deal with a very irritating rash that had developed in both my legs. While I was convinced that the rash was a side effect of the radiation therapy that I was going through, my oncologist believed that it was caused by the vitamin, mineral and herbal supplements I was taking.

My research on the internet revealed that the rash was more likely being caused by the radiation and hormonal therapies I was exposed to than the vitamin, mineral and herbal supplements I was taking.

My research also revealed that the drug that had been prescribed for me had some rather disturbing side effect. It had a significantly high possibility of inducing schizophrenia.

The internet was certainly a sea of abundance and made a big positive difference in my journey with prostate cancer. It helped empower me with knowledge and the confidence to take more ownership of my treatment program. It enabled me to take greater responsibility over my own life and health.

The fact that the diagnosis came at a time I was living in a first world country added to the list of abundant blessings that began to surface in my mind. Not only was I living in a first world country, I had just become a citizen of that country. What this meant was that I was covered by one of the best health insurance systems in the world. Apart from the medicines that I would have to buy, I was going to receive free treatment.

Coming from a third world country, I felt once again that God's timing for me was perfect. Not only was I being looked after by one of the best health care systems in the world, I was also exposed to numerous treatment options that I was free to access.

One incredible realisation that struck me as I reflected on the reality of prostate cancer in my life, was how blessed I was. As I faced the cancer and was trying to figure out how I was going to deal with it I became aware that I had numerous choices regarding the treatment approach I was going to adopt. I could go the conventional way, working with urologists, oncologists, chemotherapy and radiation therapy specialists. I could also work with specialists in the natural therapy arena. I had at my disposal naturopaths, homoeopaths, and herbalists. I could choose a combination of conventional and natural medicine.

There was an abundance of choices from which to choose. I realised how great it was to have the many choices before me. There must have been a time in the history of cancer when there was hardly any choice and it was all just one way. A diagnosis at that time meant that one would have to do just one thing, wait to die. But I had so many choices. Even if I focused on either conventional or natural medicine, I had many choices in each one of these as well.

As it turned out, I chose a combination of some conventional medicine and some natural medicine approaches to practically deal with my prostate cancer challenge. Besides my family doctor, I worked with my oncologist and her team. I also sought the services of a naturopath and a homoeopath as well as an integrative medical consultant who practiced both conventional and alternative medicine. This all worked out very well for me.

The most powerful realisation for me was that having choices in life is a sign of abundance. Because I had choices, I felt less restricted. I saw increased possibilities of dealing with the prostate cancer and this gave me hope. It was only when I began to entertain and see possibilities of defeating the cancer that I began to grow in confidence.

My mindset shifted significantly. I began to believe that all human beings lived in a world of abundance. Each person had an abundance of gifts, talents and abilities. Yet most of us chose to focus on scarcity. Most people I had met had a scarcity mentality and tended to ignore the gifts, talents and abilities they had. They felt more comfortable telling themselves that they were not gifted. They preferred to see themselves as victims of circumstances. They felt more at home letting some negative events overwhelm their lives. They would rather let negative situations and people completely delete all the good and positive that was even evident in their lives.

It became very clear to me that negative thoughts, feelings, situations and people dominated my life when I focused on them. Likewise positive thoughts, feelings, situations and people dominated my life when I focused on them. This was an irrefutable demonstration to me that whatever I chose to focus on expanded. All I had to do was make a decision about what I wanted to dominate my life. And once I had decided, all I needed to do was focus my thinking on what I had chosen. Using my mind I had the capacity to create either scarcity or abundance.

When, for example, during my cancer challenge I decided to focus my thoughts on positive things, I started by asking myself a simple question: "What should I be grateful for in my life right now?" The first time I asked myself this question my first answer was "Life". Then this led me to think of "Health" and then "People around me"; "Being in a first world country" etc. In the end I had an abundance of positive things, feelings, people and situations running my life. And I realised that this was what abundance mentality was all about. It is about making a choice to focus on the good and positive things in our lives in spite of whatever challenges we face.

For more than sixty years of my life I had problems with my thinking, my attitudes and my beliefs. I had accepted and entertained negative thinking and scarcity mentality. I had seen myself as not being good enough. I had convinced myself that other people were better than me. My self-talk was full of "I can't do this. It is impossible because I don't have this or that." I focused on impossibilities instead of possibilities. I filled my life with feelings and thoughts of lack. That was scarcity mentality.

Scarcity mentality was my initial response when I received the news of my prostate cancer diagnosis. I felt that my game of life was over and that there was nothing left for me in this world. For a while I believed that an irreversible death sentence had been passed on me . I thought my fate had been sealed. I almost let that mentality take over my life.

Fortunately for me it did not take me long to recognise, embrace and practice abundance thinking.

This happened when I decided to confront my greatest enemy - fear. It was only after breaking through the wall of my fears that I began to experience a world of possibilities. It was only then that my eyes became open enough to recognise the abundance around me.

When I received the news of my prostate cancer diagnosis, fear completely ran my life for the first five days. My greatest fear was death and this fear so terrorised and paralysed me that I could not think straight and I virtually lost all my positive creativity. However, once I started to appreciate the gifts of life and health the wall of fear started to crumble. The more abundant gifts and blessings I saw in my life the more the wall of fear melted away.

Eventually I got to a point where death no longer held any terror for me. I actually experienced a huge paradigm shift around death. I now see it as something that just is. It holds no terror for me. It holds no joy for me. It just is. The greatest lesson I learnt from this was that breaking through the fear of death brings anyone to an abundance of life.

The greatest discovery of my entire life was the realisation that my mind is the most powerful tool I have in my quest for achievement or success. My experience with prostate cancer was certainly a catalyst in bringing me to this realisation. Just by leveraging the power of my mind I moved from feelings of terror and fear to courage and hope. From seeing nothing but the darkness of death all around me, I was able to shift and to start seeing the light of life. My mind was a source of abundance.

I realised that my greatest and richest mental source of abundance was my imagination. With my imagination, I could create vivid pictures of either what I wanted and was excited about or what I was scared of. My imagination was the source of all my dreams, desires, hopes and fears of what might or might not happen. My ability to think, imagine and visualise was boundless. My only limitations were those that I placed on my own mind.

I was abundantly gifted with the capacity to conjure up in my mind pictures of the endless possibilities of what I could do with my life if I became cancer-free again. I decided that I was going to start deliberately using the God-given gift of my rich mind and imagination only for positive things. I started thinking and imagining abundance and prosperity in my life. This changed everything for me.

One big lesson I learnt from my prostate cancer experience was that whatever I spent most of my time thinking about would expand in both my mind and my life. I consciously learned that if I spent time focusing and concentrating on a certain type of thoughts, I would end up creating more thoughts of the same nature.

A concentrated focus on negative disempowering thoughts would bring about more of a negative attitude into my life. Likewise, a decision to concentrate my thinking on positive empowering thoughts would result in a positive mindset. I realised that my mind has the capacity of reproducing more of what I focus it on. What this meant and still means to me is that I have within me the power to create a host of either positive or negative thoughts and ideas. I discovered that I had the power to create abundance in my thinking and potentially in my life as well.

I remembered having read somewhere that each person has approximately between 60 000 and 90 000 thoughts a day. I wondered what kind of a day I would have if most of my thoughts were negative and fearful. I started to Imagine what a phenomenal success I would be if just half of my thoughts were positive, creative and abundant. I would become a positive influence into my own life and that of others. My attitude and behaviour would undergo a positive transformation and my life would be positively different. I resolved that I would do everything in my power to grow my positive thinking.

At first I wasn't quite sure how I was going to develop an abundance of positive thoughts, feelings and attitudes so that they would dominate my behaviour and my entire life. However, as a student of personal development I remembered that every other book I had read had mentioned the power of affirmations. For more than five years I had been a licensee of an international personal and leadership development organisation. All the programmes this organisation marketed and facilitated emphasised the power of affirmations.

I had come to understand affirmations as positive, personal present tense statements that I said to myself on a regular basis. The rationale behind affirmations was that the more I said these positive statements to myself, the more they influenced my thinking patterns and my whole mindset. Theoretically it was possible to shift my mindset from being negative to being positive. The positive thoughts conveyed by the positive statements would subliminally influence my subconscious mind and then subsequently my thinking and behaviour patterns.

I had personally used affirmations, but it had always been a half-hearted attempt. Although I had heard and read so much about affirmations I was not completely sold out on them. There was a part of me that remained sceptical and kept on telling me that I was lying to myself.

What really helped me embrace affirmations was the encouragement I got from Dr John Demartini a human behaviour specialist. He suggested that I think of my mind as a garden and that if I didn't plant flowers or vegetables or herbs in my garden, weeds were going to grow there instead. The weeds represented all the negative thoughts and ideas that I was allowing to dominate my mind. I felt highly encouraged to deliberately plant positive thoughts and ideas in the garden of my mind. Dr Demartini convinced me that affirmations were the best way to keep the garden of my mind looking and feeling beautiful.

Besides affirmations I also realised that I could inject abundant positive thinking into my life by focusing on gratitude. If I sincerely reflected on and examined my own life, there would always be things, situations and people to be grateful for. This is, fittingly, the subject of the next and final chapter of this book.

Since my prostate cancer experience, living in abundance has become a reality for me. Everything began in my mind. The biggest parts of who who I was, my mind, my thoughts and my imagination are all unlimited. There was nothing I could not think about. Who I truly was, therefore, was endless.

For the very first time in my life I could consciously and deliberately decide to attract only positive thoughts and ideas into my mind. It was no longer a very difficult thing to do. Beginning the day by thinking of the blessings in my life and expressing gratitude for them became a powerful way of inviting abundance into my life.

Beginning most of my days by reading affirmations to myself also increased my experience of abundance. Eventually I wrote down more than thirty affirmations that I still say to myself every day. This has become a habit and makes a huge positive difference in giving me a mindset of abundance during the day. I have now become more aware of the abundance that is all around me.

During my fight with prostate cancer I became a free man from the moment I stopped letting fear and lack cloud my thinking and vision. I started to believe that the more self-belief and self-confidence I had, the more abundantly I would be able to think. The idea of prosperity consciousness no longer seemed far fetched. It slowly began to make sense that we were all born for success. I felt more inclined to agree with Bob Proctor that we were all born winners in the game of life. We just needed to train ourselves to think abundantly.

As a result of my prostate cancer challenge, I realised that living an abundant and prosperous life was a result of the choices I made. I had the power to choose between prosperity thinking and poverty thinking. And my thinking in turn would influence my beliefs, attitudes and behaviour.

With my background in personal development I knew that for my attitudes and behaviour to change, my beliefs had to change.

I began to believe that if I stuck with abundance thinking long enough my health and my life in general would most likely benefit.

I had to believe that I lived in an abundant world and universe. I had to believe that in spite of my cancer challenge I qualified to have a share of that abundance. I had to believe that God was ready to bless my life with his abundant blessings if I was willing and open to receive them. I had to believe that it was possible to be healed of the prostate cancer I had been diagnosed with.

Everyday I had to challenge myself to see and believe that life was fun and rewarding despite my situation. This was not an easy thing to do. What helped me was focusing on the fact that I was not really in pain from the cancer. It was more of a diagnosed condition than a painful physical reality. What also helped me was believing that this was a blessing. I could have been in excrutiating pain, but I wasn't. So I chose to be thankful and the more thankful I was the more of a real blessing it felt.

The most interesting development was that the more I chose to look at what was good in my life, the more positive I felt. I chose to see my life as an adventure and that's what it became. I became increasingly curious, in a positive way, about what was going to turn up around the corner. When I chose to focus on looking for fun and joy in my life, they showed up most of the time.

I certainly experienced problems and difficulties especially as far as my journey with cancer was concerned. I made a choice to see those problems as challenges.

I have chosen to avoid scarcity or poverty thinking. I have stopped believing that life is hard and filled with difficulties and problems. Focusing on scarcity thinking leads me to believe that there are no opportunities. It tricks me into believing that no matter what I do – all the good ideas have been taken or that the time is not right to start new ones. This kind of thinking has invariably led me to see my situation as always hopeless and to believe that there is no point in trying. I don't want to live in that world any more. It has never served me well. It has always left me feeling stuck.

I have chosen to embrace abundance or prosperity thinking instead. I would rather believe that there are always ways to deal with every challenge or problem I meet in life. I would rather embrace the belief that there are many - countless opportunities in every aspect of my life. I would rather believe in the generosity and not the stinginess of God or the Universe.

I choose to believe that there are many countless opportunities in all areas of my life. At the time of my diagnosis I chose to see opportunities for abundant health. I still see myself today as a person who is blessed with good health.

I now know that God has always given and continues to give me many opportunities to build new and loving relationships. I have the capacity to love others and to experience love from God and from those people close to me. Believing that I am abundantly surrounded by love has led me to a place where my sense of value and self-worth has gone up. I have the capacity to open my life to this and to co-create these love opportunities.

I have also become aware of an abundance of opportunities to study, learn, grow and advance myself. I am surrounded by an abundance of information. If I wanted to become an expert in any area of life, there is a lot of free information on the internet – YouTube, websites, subscriptions, newsletters, blogs etc. I can start with a few books that I peronally have and then get more books from bookshops and libraries.

I am thinking abundantly when I acknowledge that I have all the resources I need to resolve and deal with whatever challenges come my way. Whenever I choose to believe that I can create solutions to whatever problems come my way, I always find a way. I become rich in new ideas.

There are certainly times when subconsciously I start telling myself that life is tough. And sure enough moving forward becomes a struggle. However, I have now learnt to ask myself: "Is thinking like this serving me in any way?" The answer that comes back is always "No!" Every time I stack the odds against myself I don't win. I have to get out of my own way.

Abundance thinking is consciously choosing to think that I am surrounded by opportunities to live a happy and fulfilling life. During my journey with cancer this was a choice I made every day.

We live in a land of countless opportunities, but no one will just hand them to us. We first have to believe that they exist. Then we have to go out and look for them and when we find them, we have to make good use of them.

Abundance thinking is believing that a challenging situation is only temporary. It is a conviction on my part that I am bigger than the problem I face. It is believing that I have a greater chance of winning than losing.

Abundance mentality takes full responsibility for our own success and failure. It says that I am one hundred percent responsible for the way my life is now and for the way it will be in future. My success or failure is my responsibility.

I have total conviction that I am surrounded by abundance. It has been and continues to be worthwhile to always look for the good in my life. Despite life's inevitable challenges it is a worthwhile cause to strive daily to create a heaven for myself here on earth. I would rather shoot for the stars. If I miss the stars at least I will have the moon as a prize.

Affirmations: I LIVE IN ABUNDANCE

- *I am created in the image of an abundant and infinite source.*
- *My abundant and infinite source gives me immeasurable value.*
- *I see challenges as hidden sources of power that help me to see my true value.*

- *I experience my greatest wealth in the way I choose to use my mind.*
- *I use my mind's power to enrich myself in all ways.*
- *I daily entertain thoughts that empower me and increase my wealth.*
- *I grow wealthier every day as I experience more and more of God's blessings in my life.*
- *I am a wonderfully and beautifully created human being with immeasurable value.*
- *My worth and value grows every time I touch and positively impact someone's life.*
- *I see failures and mistakes as sources of internal wealth which leave me stronger.*

CHAPTER 8

I CHOOSE AN ATTITUDE OF GRATITUDE

*The more you recognise and express gratitude
for the things you have, the more things you
will have to express gratitude for.*
Zig Ziglar - 1926-2012, Author and Speaker

It's all so familiar and you take it for granted,
your gifts and talents and the good of others.
The beauty around you, you hardly notice,
absorbed in your faults and those of others.
Seems natural to blame, complain, whinge, mourn
and create an energy field of negative thoughts.

Your thoughts and feelings are shaped by focus,
even your actions when eventually they happen.
Make up your mind what holds your focus.
Think of all the good that you've seen happen.
Think of all the gifts and talents in your possession.
Then choose gratitude and sincerely express it.

Listen to the magical sound of "Thank You!"
To whom and for what makes no difference.
Many situations and people have enriched you,
so just say "Thank you!" and make a difference.
Your life will be richer and so will theirs,
As more doors start opening all over.

Be glad and grateful for your very existence.
Your life and health don't take for granted;
your achievements since coming into existence;
the family and friends you have been granted;
the blessing and gift of yet another day.
To be thankful, what a feeling, what a gift to have!

To say 'Thank you' is a way of attracting
more of the things for which you're grateful
Appreciation creates a magnetic force in you,
And the more you do it the stronger the force
That brings more blessings that bring more gratitude
That fill your life only with the things you love.

When on the 1st of March 2011 my urologist told me "You have prostate cancer", there was sudden darkness in my mind. I experienced what felt like a blackout. Momentarily, I could not think. I felt totally confused. As I regained full consciousness of where I was and what was happening, I felt a surge of fear. I also felt anger and resentment rising in my heart and mind.

Why was this happening to me? Why had God visited me with the curse of all curses – cancer. Why had he allowed this to happen to me?" What had I done wrong to deserve this?

Had the active cancer cells been triggered off by the stressful experience of relocating to Australia? In 2006 my wife and I had sold and given away virtually all our earthly possessions and left our country of birth, Zimbabwe, where I had lived the entire 58 years of my life. I felt that I had lost everything I had worked for my entire life.

And settling down in Australia had not been easy at all. It all meant that I had to start all over again, especially as far as my career was concerned. From being a school principal and businessman in Zimbabwe, I found myself doing menial jobs in the factories of Sydney, Australia. I found myself cleaning offices and factories. I had to do anything to put some food on the table and provide a roof over our heads. It was a traumatic experience that had left some mental, psychological and possibly physical scars.

So as I now tried to come to terms with the prostate cancer diagnosis, the most vivid picture of myself that I first saw was that of a victim. From the very moment I decided to leave my country of birth I became a victim. I started to blame the circumstances that had led me to make that decision. The economic and political situation was to blame and so were the politicians who were responsible for the economic and political administration of the country. I felt totally convinced that had it not been for those people and circumstances I would not have become a victim of prostate cancer

For the first five days after my diagnosis, I experienced an isolation I had never felt before. I felt deeply unloved and very lonely. I felt abandoned by God and the rest of the world. They had chosen to isolate me as a victim. My negative mindset stripped me of any reason to live. There was nothing for me to smile about and appreciate about myself and the world that surrounded me.

If, on the sixth day, I had not remembered that I was a life coach, I would have gracefully accepted that my life was through. The awakening of the coach saved my life. It reminded me of who I was. It led me to having long conversations or "coaching sessions" with myself.

The awakening of the coach in me helped me realise that I was a co-creator with God of all that is good. Just as I had planted the spirit of hope, determination and confidence into the lives of my coaching clients, I had the power to do the same for myself. This emotionally and spiritually empowered me to move forward. I started to question my own negativity and victim mentality.

It was all very well spending time entertaining myself with the fact that I was a cancer victim. I had identified God, other people and circumstances to blame for the way my life was. I could justifiably complain, whinge and moan every moment and day of the rest of my life. It was not difficult to find reasons to do so. I had been diagnosed with an aggressive type of prostate cancer. This was a real threat to my life. This was the most negative and life-threatening development in my entire 63 years in this world.

I had trusted God to take care of me and protect me from such enemies as cancer. I had prayed for that frequently. But God didn't seem to have done a good job of it. I felt justified to ask "why", to blame him and to see myself as a poor and unfortunate victim. I could justifiably feel sorry for myself for the rest of my life.

But then how was this way of thinking going to serve me? If I continued to think in this way where would that lead me to? How was it going to improve the quality of my life? I could find reasons to blame God. I could complain that other people were not sufficiently there for me. I could justifiably blame circumstances that I felt had contributed in bringing about my prostate cancer status. But then how was that attitude going to help me fight the cancer that had invaded my body? How was that going to help me prolong my life even by just another day, week or month? How was that going to give me a better quality of life before I died whenever that was going to be?

I decided to abandon the victim mentality attitude. I could now see more clearly that the more I entertained this victim mentality, the more of a victim I felt, the less progress I made and the more miserable, unhappy and anxious I became. That attitude led me to feeling weighed down physically and psychologically by the challenge I faced. It drove my spirits down into deep despair, hopelessness and helplessness. Was this what I wanted for myself?

Absolutely not!

I began to realise that unless I changed the way I looked at life my situation was just going to get worse. I was simply going to raise the levels of my negative energy. I would have chosen to be unhappy, miserable and stressed for the rest of my life. That would certainly not serve me. It, clearly, was not in my best interest.

The cancer that I faced was my worst and most formidable enemy. A weak and negative attitude would give me no chance at all to defeat this enemy. It would be like a virus. It would stress me and weaken my immune system. Only a highly positive fighting spirit stood any chance of helping me to successfully fight this prostate cancer battle. It was an antidote that might open new life possibilities for me.

I became aware that I had the power to create hell on earth for myself. That power lay in my mind and how I chose to use it. I could also use the same mind-power to create a heaven on earth for myself. I had the power of choice which I could use either way. At that point I vividly became aware that it was actually up to me.

Was it going to be heaven or hell? It was difficult to visualise a blissful heaven for myself especially with prostate cancer. However, I was very clear in my mind that I wanted to be as far away from hell on earth as I could. I would rather be halfway between hell and heaven than spend the rest of my life in the depressing clutches of hell.

For the first time since my diagnosis I saw in my mind the clear choice that I had between "hope" and "despair". Whenever I was going to die, what path was I choosing to get there? Was it a path filled with hope or was it a path strewn with thorns of despair? I had to decide.

It was at this point that I made up my mind once and for all to face the prostate cancer with as positive a mindset as I could muster. I knew it wasn't going to be easy. It was going to be an uphill struggle. I would be confronting the reality that I had prostate cancer. I would be facing the cancer itself and all the inevitable challenges that came with my efforts to overcome it. I knew that whatever treatment programme I chose, it wasn't going to be a walk in the park.

Thinking about these challenges was a scary and daunting experience. I felt tempted to follow the path of least resistance. I could just surrender to the prostate cancer and let it take over and completely run my life. After all it was now a reality for me. Of all the diseases that afflicted the human body cancer had the worst reputation. It had inflicted terror in the minds and bodies of hundreds of thousands of people worldwide. Physically and mentally stronger people than me, including my two brothers, had buckled and died in the face of cancer. Who was I to think that I could face it and succeed using a positive mindset? Was I not fooling myself?

Such thoughts and questions would drive me down into a state of depression and I would feel stuck there for a while. What always brought me back to some form of control again was reminding myself of my unique identity. I was David Pasipanodya. I was unique and with no comparison. I was not like any one of those other millions. I was not my two deceased brothers either. I was facing this challenge with an identity, personality and mindset that was totally unique to me.

It was not about changing circumstances and people out there – I couldn't change them anyway. It was all about changing me. It was also about keeping myself positively centred. How I was choosing to see the situation would either empower or disempower me.

I asked myself this empowering question. "Who would I go to right now to get advice, coaching and guidance about this challenge I am facing right now? Whose ideas would empower me to face the prostate cancer with a positive attitude?"

"Dr John Demartini" was my answer. Dr Demartini is a world class human behavioural expert, bestselling author and international speaker.

I had attended many of his talks and seminars including his signature programme *"The Breakthrough Experience."* I had also read quite a few of his books. I distinctly recalled his book *"The Gratitude Effect".* I vividly remembered him saying in the book that there were blessings even in the greatest of adversities. He had come up with a long list of more than 60 blessings that he saw resulting from the devastating 9/11 event of 2001 which d. Arguing that there is no crisis without a blessing, he also came up with a list of the good things that had come out of the South East Asian Tsunami of 2004 which killed at least 225 000 people. He encouraged his readers, and I was one of them, to look for, find and be grateful for the blessings that surrounded us even as we faced the greatest challenges of our lives.

Facing my cancer diagnosis crisis, I initially found Dr Demartini's arguments too superficial and unrealistic. This was an unprecedented personal crisis that directly threatened my life. I had stage 4 prostate cancer, which most likely had already spread to other parts of my body. What blessing could possibly be found in that? Facing this challenge there was nothing to be grateful for in my life.

However, I trusted Dr Demartini and valued his views highly. I had gone through a powerful personal transformation by attending his signature programme: *"The Breakthrough Experience"* in July 2010. I had learnt to embrace and completely forgive one particular individual I had vowed to hate all the way to my grave.

The process that Dr John Demartini led me through during *"The Breakthrough Experience"* gave me the most powerful breakthrough I had ever had in my entire life. The highlight of the two-day seminar involved getting me to closely examine the person I disliked most in the world. I did this using a method and a process that ended with me having a very deep appreciation of that person's role in my life. The experience left me in an emotionally tear-filled state where I felt at peace with myself and my former adversary. I also had deep feelings of gratitude, forgiveness and unconditional love for someone that I used to hate with a passion.

"The Breakthrough Experience" left me a free man at peace with the world. It significantly deepened my faith in God. I became significantly less judgemental. My life was transformed.

So as I reflected about my prostate cancer diagnosis, Dr John Demartini came to my mind. Maybe I could trust him. Maybe he could help me to positively face the life-threatening challenge before me. Maybe his views on how to positively handle a crisis could give me the breakthrough I needed.

I had nothing to lose and there was the possibility of gaining a completely new perspective on my situation. I felt challenged to refer to Dr Demartini's book *"The Gratitude Effect"* and to look for the blessings in my cancer situation.

I thought to myself: "How would it be if I shifted my focus? Instead of spending a lot of time thinking about myself as a helpless and powerless victim, what if I focused my mind on thinking and being thankful about what I have, the good and positive around me? Could there be some blessings hidden in the "Tsunami" of the prostate cancer that I faced?"

These thoughts actually made me feel curious. It would be interesting to take my mind in that direction. However, this was not at all easy to do. It was far easier for me to continue to see myself as a victim and to indulge in self-pity. Inside my body was the biggest threat I had ever faced in my entire life. How could I possibly ignore that?

I decided not to ignore but rather to embrace it and find ways I could use it in my favour. I would have to coach myself just as I would a client.

Firstly, I had to accept and acknowledge the reality of the challenge facing me. The tests and diagnosis had been done and I had prostate cancer in my body. That was now a medical fact. This was reality and nothing was going to change that. It was what it was and I had to accept it.

Secondly, I assessed the situation by asking myself these empowering questions. What exactly is the situation? How do I feel about it? How am I choosing to respond to this situation?

Well, I had been diagnosed with an aggressive type of prostate cancer. I felt scared, angry and confused. After initially feeling helpless and seeing myself as a victim I now wanted to empower myself to find ways to effectively deal with the challenge. If at all I could, I wanted to win this battle with prostate cancer. I was choosing to look for solutions rather than surrender to the challenge.

Finally. I chose to empower myself. I asked myself these questions "What one good thing can I find in this situation? What is it that I can choose to be grateful for in my life right now? What one thing can I see in my life right now that is positive? What could I possibly smile about and say 'thank you' to God for? What is there to be grateful for and appreciate in my life right now?"

Initially those questions seemed to block my thinking and I felt stuck for a while. Could there be anything good that I could be grateful for in my cancer diagnosis? Then, as I spoke to myself in an attempt to answer my own question, a light bulb flashed in my mind.

"I guess I can choose to be grateful that I am alive. I have the gift of life. I am not dead."

Then almost immediately I said to myself: "I also have the gift of health. Physically, I am not sick." Although I had been diagnosed with prostate cancer, I was not feeling any physical pain yet. The pain and suffering I was experiencing was in my mind. And it was because I was choosing to see myself as a poor helpless victim. My enemy was actually my own mind!

"Well, this is incredible! I have something to be grateful for! I have to thank God for the gift of life and health! I could very easily have been diagnosed when I was already in pain with the cancer. But I am feeling perfectly healthy and this in itself gives me a fighting chance against the cancer that has invaded my body. It would have been much harder for me to put up a fight if I was in pain."

I was clearly choosing thoughts, ideas and arguments which supported a positive outcome in my battle with prostate cancer. I was giving myself reasons to be brave and courageous. I was building confidence for survival.

The realisation that I was making choices about what to focus on brought about a big mind shift. I was actually a host to the thoughts that were visiting my mind. Whatever these thoughts were, they were my guests. If I chose to make them feel welcome and to entertain them, then they would become comfortable, feel at home and start running my life. So if I chose to entertain negative thoughts my life would soon be dominated by fear, anxiety, worry and depression and I would soon be living in hell.

Is this what I wanted? Certainly not!

On the other hand, if they were positive thoughts that I chose to entertain, then my mind would soon be dominated by hope, courage, confidence in the future and the possibilities of a more empowered life. This was my hope. I would love to be in this space.

The very realisation that I could choose what thoughts to entertain was very empowering to me. I actually had the gift of choice. I also realised that to be able to pick out what thoughts I was going to entertain I would have to be connected to myself. I would have to be at peace with myself. I would have to be alert and aware of what I was thinking. I would have to observe myself thinking. I would literally have to think about what I was thinking. If there was turmoil in my mind, I would not be able to have that awareness.

At that point, I actually felt grateful for that peace and for that ability to connect with myself. I was asking myself questions and finding some answers to those questions. Yes, this was something positive happening in my life. It was a very interesting place to be. It was a place of growth.

I made a commitment to myself that I would strive to entertain positive thoughts of life and health as much as I could. I would also avoid, as much as I could, thoughts that would destroy my peace and bring about mental turmoil.

For the first time since hearing about my diagnosis, I felt empowered. I felt positive. I felt energised.

It was all about me and not the cancer. I and not the cancer had to choose how I wanted to live my life from then on. The quality of life that I was going to live was going to be determined by how I chose to live my life and not by focusing on the fact that I had prostate cancer. My choice of mindset was the key. I had to adopt a positive attitude! If I really focused on it I could actually be bigger than the cancer that had invaded my body.

In a strange way, this was one of the most empowering moments in my entire life. Knowing that I had prostate cancer gave me a power, vision, focus and sense of purpose that I never thought I possessed. As I saw the preciousness of life in a completely new dimension, I felt challenged and at the same time energised to value each moment of my life more than I had ever done before. I realised that life was a treasure which I needed to hold in my hand, feel its pulse each moment that I lived it. I had to give it the value that it truly deserved and focus on making a positive difference in this world that I was so privileged to live in.

As I experienced this deep sense of gratitude, I remembered that many of my high school and university friends had passed on. Some had died in road accidents, some of cancer and yet others of HIV/AIDS, and other diseases. Some of these colleagues had been my very best friends. I had lost two brothers to cancer. And here I was fully alive and healthy, playing victim and worrying myself to death because of just a diagnosis.

What a gift it was to be alive!

I was facing a real possibility of losing my life to cancer and yet I felt the beauty and magnificence of life like never before. Being alive and healthy gave me the best chance possible to fight the cancer that had invaded my body. I could already have been very sick and experiencing a lot of pain from the cancer. But thank God, I was not! I literally went down on my knees and whispered: "Thank you God for the wonderful gift of life and health!"

I felt tears of gratitude flow down my face. I was not hopeless and helpless. My life and my health were fully available to me. It was all up to me to decide how best to use these gifts, not just for my own benefit but for other people as well. I decided then that I would devote the rest of my life to making a positive difference in the world around me. That was also the point where I made the decision to write this book.

Becoming aware of and being grateful for the amazing gifts of life and health was a turning point. It opened the floodgates for my mind to see and be grateful for many more gifts and blessings that I had never imagined. The more things I saw in my life and expressed gratitude for, the more things appeared for which I could express further gratitude. This experience significantly strengthened my belief in the law of attraction. I am now totally convinced that by being grateful, I attract more things to be grateful for.

This experience provided a very powerful lifeline for me. I have since then always remembered what a gift life and health were to me. It was a transformational experience that has given me a lifetime of daily counting my blessings. It gave me an attitude that opened my eyes to a new reality of increasingly and daily growing favours and blessings.

Strangely enough, the more grateful I felt, the less scared of death I was. I discovered that there was power in gratitude and that if I spent more time focusing on what was good in my life and asking myself the right questions, I would empower myself.

As a result of this experience I now totally believe in the power of gratitude. I sincerely believe that the more grateful I am the more blessings and gifts I get. When I think of giving and receiving I am now aware that this also involves giving gratitude. If I give gratitude I open my life to receiving more from the universe, from God.

Gratitude consciousness has now become a part of how I think and behave. I now have a growing written list of things in my life that I am grateful for. I am developing a habit of daily reading this list and adding to it whenever I identify a new blessing, opportunity or gift that has recently arrived in my life. I sincerely believe that every person on the face of the earth will benefit and grow significantly by making gratitude a central focus of their lives.

Since that experience I have always looked for and found the good in all the challenges I have had. Every time I face a challenging situation and I take the time to look for anything positive in that situation, I always find it. And when I find it, I express gratitude for it and I add it to my list of gratitudes. This has made my life an amazing adventure and an incredible journey.

I have found that every challenge I have faced has contained seeds of growth and left me a better person than I was before. It has been and continues to be an amazing journey.

When we come face to face with life's inevitable challenges, we have the freedom to choose how to respond. We can choose to become disempowered by entertaining fear, worry and anxiety. We can also empower ourselves by choosing courage, growth and above all GRATITUDE. And when we choose gratitude, we come face to face with the abundant generosity through which the God of the universe speaks into our lives.

Affirmations: I CHOOSE AN ATTITUDE OF GRATITUDE

- *I am deeply grateful for the gifts of life and health.*
- *I trust life and feel grateful for all the events and people that surround me.*
- *I focus my mind on being thankful for the good things in my life.*
- *I live with gratitude by looking for the good in every challenge that I face.*
- *Instead of focusing on the obstacles I look for and find solutions to my challenges.*
- *I feel grateful for the awareness that my life is a priceless treasure that I need to deeply value.*
- *I am living a blessed life. The more grateful I am, the more things I find to be grateful for.*
- *The more things I find to be grateful for the less fears and regrets I have.*
- *In the face of life's challenges I empower myself by choosing courage, growth and gratitude.*
- *I choose gratitude and I experience abundant generosity from my source of supply.*

Acknowledgements

To Nurse my amazing wife. Your unconditional love has been a source of strength and the growing confidence that I have developed on my journey to become an author.

The more you believed in me, the more I believed in myself and the infinite potential that I have. The spiritual journey that we have shared and walked together has inspired me to believe that sharing my thoughts through writing was an important part of my God-given mission and purpose in life. Thank you for allowing me to wonder, sometimes at odd hours and places, into my own world of reading and writing.

To my five children Elizabeth, Tanaka, Tatenda, Tadiwa and Tarongerwa. I thank you for your lives. You represent legacy to me and you are the reason why I wrote this book. I have always wanted you to know a lot more about me than I ever had the courage to talk about or model for you. I hope that this book will fill that gap and help you to know, understand and appreciate what's going on in my head. Thank you for your encouragement.

A special thank you to my daughter Tadiwa. You inspired the cover design and layout for this book. I appreciate.

Thank you Puwai Mpofu for your energetic enthusiasm in putting the final touches to the cover design.

My acknowledgements would be incomplete if I did not mention Laurens Boel. Virtually half my age, your voracious appetite to become an author was a great source of inspiration for me. When you coached me and showed me how you had done it, you cemented my belief that I could do it too. I am grateful.

To Frank Nunan my editor, thank you for your patience and for helping to put this book together. I couldn't have done it without you.

Finally I am grateful to those many people who, once I had told them I was writing a book, persistently asked me "when is the book coming out?" You taught me the most powerful lessons in persistence.

www.ingramcontent.com/pod-product-compliance
Lightning Source LLC
Chambersburg PA
CBHW061822040426
42447CB00012B/2769